THE
FASTING
Advantage

Copyright © 2024 by Thando Sibanda

Published by Four Rivers Media

All rights reserved. No portion of this book may be reproduced, stored in a retrieval system, or transmitted in any form or by any means—electronic, mechanical, photocopy, recording, scanning, or other—except for brief quotations in critical reviews or articles, without prior written permission of the author.

Unless otherwise specified, all Scripture quotations are taken from the New King James Version®. Copyright © 1982 by Thomas Nelson. Used by permission. All rights reserved. | Scripture quotations marked ESV are from The ESV® Bible (The Holy Bible, English Standard Version®), copyright © 2001 by Crossway, a publishing ministry of Good News Publishers. Used by permission. All rights reserved. | Scripture quotations marked NIV are taken from the Holy Bible, New International Version®, NIV®. Copyright © 1973, 1978, 1984, 2011 by Biblica, Inc.™ Used by permission of Zondervan. All rights reserved worldwide. www.zondervan.com. The "NIV" and "New International Version" are trademarks registered in the United States Patent and Trademark Office by Biblica, Inc.™ | Scripture quotations marked WBT are taken from the Western Bible Translation, Copyright © 2013, 2014. Used by permission.

For foreign and subsidiary rights, contact the author.

Cover design by Sara Young
Cover photo by Shift Focus Photography

ISBN: 978-1-964794-29-7   1 2 3 4 5 6 7 8 9 10

Printed in the United States of America

WHAT PEOPLE ARE SAYING ABOUT
THE FASTING ADVANTAGE

In a time when the noise of modern life often drowns out the profound practices of spiritual growth, Dr. Thando Sibanda brings us *The Fasting Advantage*—a transformative guide that reconnects the ancient discipline of fasting with the modern believer's journey. Seamlessly integrating biblical wisdom with scientific insights, this book unveils fasting as a powerful tool for both spiritual renewal and physical vitality.

Dr. Sibanda's approach is not only deeply theological but also refreshingly practical, making it accessible to those just beginning to explore fasting and equally enriching for seasoned practitioners. His balance of personal anecdotes, scriptural grounding, and actionable advice creates a compelling invitation to embrace fasting as a lifestyle of alignment with God's purposes.

The Fasting Advantage is more than a book; it's a call to rediscover the intersection of faith, discipline, and holistic transformation. I wholeheartedly recommend this work to anyone seeking to deepen their walk with God and unlock the profound blessings of fasting.

—Martijn Van Tilborgh
CEO, AVAIL

Dr. Thando delivers a masterpiece with his latest book *The Fasting Advantage*. Throughout these pages he offers biblical insights and profound discoveries as he unpacks the secrets to this sacred discipline. I highly recommend you read this book and unveil the powerful principles that are sure to revolutionize your spiritual journey.

—Chris Sonksen
Pastor/Speaker/Author/Coach
Founder & CEO, Church Boom

This book is a must-read! It is timely for our generation and ought to be a companion of anyone who desires to live a healthy life, lead with power, fulfill their God-given vision, and experience a deeper walk with God.

Allow these powerful revelations and compilation of balanced research by Dr. Thando Sibanda, a passionate worshipper, and an intellectual powerhouse, to guide you to what really matters. *The Fasting Advantage* will enlighten, educate, and equip you for growth and success.

—Kiplin Batchelor
Public Relations Director
Managing Editor: *The Voice Magazine*
Christ for the Nations Institute

THE FASTING *Advantage*

Unlocking the Spiritual
and Scientific Power of Fasting

DR. THANDO SIBANDA

The Ultimate Blueprint for Fasting:
Bridging Faith, Science, and Personal Transformation

OTHER BOOKS AND RESOURCES BY
DR THANDO SIBANDA

The Fasting Companion

The Fasting Companion Masterclass

Pathway to Renewal

The Winning Mindset

The Fasting Companion app

Coffee Is Only for Closers

To my beloved parents, Jonah and Alice Sibanda, whose faith and wisdom laid the foundation of my life.

Thank you for raising thirteen children with unwavering dedication and teaching us to walk the ancient pathways of the Lord. Through your lives, you showed us what it means to contact, contain, and convey the essence of Yahweh. Your commitment to timeless biblical principles and your steadfast love for God has shaped us all, leaving an indelible legacy that stretches across generations.

This book is a testament to the seeds you planted—of faith, resilience, and reverence— that continue to grow and bear fruit.

CONTENTS

PRELUDE 13
THE POWER OF RENEWAL 15

PART 1. THE SPIRITUALITY OF FASTING 19

CHAPTER 1. FASTING IN HISTORY 21
CHAPTER 2. THE CALL TO BIBLICAL FASTING 27
CHAPTER 3. THE RELATIONSHIP BETWEEN
PRAYER AND FASTING 35
CHAPTER 4. FASTING PROFILES
IN THE BIBLICAL NARRATIVE 43
CHAPTER 5. FASTING IN THE NEW TESTAMENT:
JESUS AND THE EARLY CHURCH 55
CHAPTER 6. THE POWER OF CORPORATE FASTING .. 63
CHAPTER 7. PREPARING FOR YOUR FAST 71
CHAPTER 8. OPTIMIZING YOUR FAST 81
CHAPTER 9. ENDURING IN YOUR FAST 91
CHAPTER 10. BREAKING YOUR FAST 101
CHAPTER 11. SUSTAINING THE SPIRITUAL AND
PHYSICAL GAINS OF FASTING 107

PART 2. THE SCIENCE OF FASTING 115

CHAPTER 12. UNDERSTANDING THE SCIENCE
OF FASTING 117
CHAPTER 13. NEUROTHEOLOGY: THE INTERSECTION
OF MIND, BODY, AND SPIRIT 127
CHAPTER 14. WHAT ACTUALLY HAPPENS
TO YOUR BODY WHEN YOU FAST? 137

CHAPTER 15.	COMMON SYMPTOMS WHILE FASTING	. 149
PART 3.	**EMBRACING THE LIFESTYLE OF FASTING**	.157
CHAPTER 16.	FASTING AS A LIFESTYLE	.161
CHAPTER 17.	THE POWER OF COMMUNITY IN FASTING	.167
CHAPTER 18.	FASTING AND SPIRITUAL WARFARE	.177
EPILOGUE		183
ENDNOTES............................		189

> "It is the glory of God to conceal a thing, but the honor of kings is to search out a matter."
> —King Solomon, 700 BC
>
> Proverbs 25:2 (WBT)

PRELUDE

In an age where instant gratification reigns and the concept of waiting seems foreign, the ancient practice of fasting stands as a beacon of countercultural wisdom. Fasting, once a cornerstone of spiritual discipline across various traditions, has been misunderstood and often overlooked in our modern world. Yet, it is a practice that has the potential to transform not just our spiritual lives, but our physical and mental well-being as well.

The Fasting Advantage invites you into a journey that transcends the mere act of abstaining from food. It calls you to engage in a holistic experience that connects the spiritual and the physical, the ancient and the modern. Through the pages of this book, you will discover the profound power of fasting—not as a relic of the past but as a vibrant and vital discipline for today.

This book is more than just a guide; it is a roadmap to deeper intimacy with God, greater spiritual insight, and enhanced physical health. As an advocate of fasting who comes from a family legacy of prayer and fasting, this book is very real for me as I am familiar with the experiences outlined in the whole journey of the twenty-one-day fasting protocol. Whether you are new to fasting or have practiced it for years, *The Fasting Advantage* offers fresh perspectives and practical strategies that will enrich your fasting journey.

As you delve into the chapters ahead, you will explore fasting through the lens of Scripture, learn about the latest scientific research on its benefits, and be inspired by historical and modern-day revivals where fasting played a pivotal role. You will also find answers to common questions, practical tips for every stage of the fasting process, and encouragement to make fasting a regular part of your spiritual routine.

In a world that is constantly clamoring for our attention, fasting helps us to pause, to listen, and to realign our lives with God's purposes. It strips away the noise and distractions, allowing us to focus on what truly matters. This book will equip you to harness the power of fasting, not just as an occasional practice but as a lifestyle that can lead to lasting transformation.

As you turn these pages, my prayer is that you will be inspired to embrace fasting with a renewed sense of purpose and expectation. *May The Fasting Advantage* empower you to experience breakthroughs in your spiritual journey, deepen your relationship with God, and witness the incredible benefits that fasting can bring to every area of your life.

Welcome to the journey. Let the transformation begin.

—Dr Thando Sibanda

THE POWER OF RENEWAL

"For Renewal, Snakes Shed Their Old Skin, Eagles Pluck Out Their Feathers. Humans Fast."

This powerful statement captures the essence of renewal, drawing on the natural world's wisdom to illustrate a profound spiritual truth. Just as snakes and eagles undergo significant physical transformations to ensure their survival and growth, humans engage in fasting to achieve both spiritual and physiological renewal.

SPIRITUAL RENEWAL: SHEDDING THE OLD, EMBRACING THE NEW

In the natural world, snakes regularly shed their old skin in a process known as ecdysis. This act is vital for their growth and survival, allowing them to remove parasites, heal from injuries, and make room for new, healthy skin. Spiritually, humans must also shed the "old skin"—the habits, sins, and mindsets that hinder our relationship with God. Fasting is a spiritual discipline that facilitates this shedding process. It is a time of introspection and purification, where we intentionally lay aside the distractions and excesses of life to focus on God.

Just as the snake's shedding allows it to move forward unencumbered, fasting enables us to break free from spiritual stagnation. It creates space for God to work in our hearts, removing the barriers that prevent us from growing closer to Him. Through fasting, we can experience a deep spiritual renewal—a rebirth of sorts—that empowers us to embrace the new things God has in store for us.

PHYSIOLOGICAL RENEWAL: STRENGTHENING THE BODY AND MIND

Eagles, on the other hand, go through a process called molting, where they pluck out their old, worn-out feathers and old beaks to make way for new growth. This process is painful and leaves the eagle vulnerable, but it is essential for the bird to maintain its strength and ability to soar at great heights. Similarly, fasting has profound physiological benefits that contribute to the renewal of the body and mind.

When we fast, our bodies undergo a series of remarkable changes. Fasting triggers cellular repair processes, reduces inflammation, and promotes detoxification. It gives the digestive system a much-needed break, allowing the body to redirect its energy toward healing and regeneration. On a deeper level, fasting can also enhance mental clarity, improve focus, and elevate mood by balancing hormones and neurotransmitters.

Just as the eagle emerges from molting with renewed strength and vitality, fasting helps us renew our physical bodies, preparing us to face life's challenges with greater resilience and vigor.

THE SYNERGY OF SPIRITUAL AND PHYSIOLOGICAL RENEWAL

Fasting is unique in that it brings together both spiritual and physiological renewal in a powerful synergy. As we deny our bodies, we strengthen our spirits; as we clear our minds, we open our hearts to God's voice. This dual renewal process enables us to become more attuned to God's will, more disciplined in our daily lives, and more equipped to fulfill our divine purpose.

Through fasting, we are invited into a sacred rhythm of letting go and receiving, of shedding and growing, of weakening the flesh to strengthen the spirit. It is a time-honored practice that not only transforms us from the inside out but also aligns us more closely with the natural order of renewal that God has woven into the fabric of creation.

PART 1

The Spirituality of Fasting

CHAPTER 1

FASTING IN HISTORY
How Fasting Has Shaped Spiritual Disciplines Throughout History

FASTING IN THE ABRAHAMIC RELIGIONS: A SACRED PRACTICE

In a world where the rhythms of life have become frenetic and consumption is celebrated, the concept of abstaining from food can seem almost alien. Yet, fasting is one of the most ancient practices known to humanity. It has been embraced across different cultures, religions, and societies for thousands of years. From Biblical ancestors to other ancient cultures, fasting has been a channel of ascendancy and renewal.

Fasting may seem countercultural today, but this very act of countering the culture is what gives fasting its power. As we journey through this chapter, we will explore the roots of fasting, uncover its evolution through history, and understand how this ancient practice has shaped civilizations and spiritual disciplines alike. By the end of this chapter, you'll gain a new appreciation for fasting—not just as a religious obligation, but as a transformative practice that has stood the test of time.

The Earliest Records of Fasting: Where It All Began

To truly understand the significance of fasting, we must travel back in time. The Abrahamic religions—Judaism, Christianity, and Islam—have all embraced fasting as a sacred practice, each with its own unique traditions and significance.

In Judaism, fasting is most notably observed during Yom Kippur, the Day of Atonement, when Jews fast for twenty-five hours as a means of repentance and spiritual cleansing. Fasting is also observed on other days of mourning and remembrance, such as Tisha B'av, which commemorates the destruction of the First and Second Temples in Jerusalem.

Christianity, as we will explore further in later chapters, has a rich tradition of fasting rooted in both the Old and New Testaments. From corporate national fasts, congregational fasts, as well as individual fasts like the forty-day fast that Jesus undertook. Fasting in Christianity is seen as a way to draw closer to God, seek spiritual guidance, and cultivate self-discipline.

In Islam, fasting is one of the five pillars of the faith, most prominently observed during the holy month of Ramadan. Muslims fast from dawn until sunset for twenty-nine to thirty days, abstaining from food, drink, and other physical needs. The fast is seen as an act of worship, a means of developing self-control, and an opportunity for spiritual reflection and renewal.

Each of these traditions emphasizes the spiritual significance of fasting, a way to draw closer to God, purify the soul, and develop a deeper sense of humility and gratitude. Fasting in the Abrahamic religions is not just a personal practice; it is a communal one, bringing people together in a shared act of devotion and faith.

As we move forward in history, we find ourselves in ancient Greece, a society that placed a high value on the mind and intellect. Here, fasting took on a new dimension. Greek philosophers, including the likes of Socrates, Plato, and Pythagoras, were known to practice fasting as a means of enhancing mental clarity and spiritual insight. In a world where the pursuit of knowledge was paramount, fasting was seen as a tool to sharpen the mind, heighten awareness, and cultivate self-discipline.

Pythagoras, the renowned mathematician and philosopher, required his students to fast before they could be admitted into his school. He believed that fasting was essential for mental and spiritual preparation, allowing the mind to transcend the physical and connect with deeper truths. This belief was rooted in the idea that the body and the soul were intrinsically connected; by disciplining the body, one could also discipline the soul.

Fasting in Early Christianity: The Desert Fathers and Monastic Traditions

As Christianity began to spread, the practice of fasting became deeply embedded in the life of the early Church. The Desert Fathers, a group of early Christian hermits and monks living in the deserts of Egypt, were known for their rigorous fasting practices. They believed that fasting was essential for overcoming the desires of the flesh, growing in spiritual strength, and drawing closer to God.

The monastic tradition, which emerged from these early hermits, also placed a strong emphasis on fasting. Monks and nuns would often fast as part of their daily routine, abstaining from food for extended periods to focus on prayer, meditation, and spiritual growth. Fasting was seen as a way to cultivate virtues such as humility, patience, and self-control.

The practice of fasting in early Christianity was not just about personal piety; it was also about communal discipline. The early Church established specific days for fasting, such as Wednesdays and Fridays, to commemorate the betrayal and crucifixion of Jesus. These communal fasts were a way for believers to unite in their devotion and sacrifice, strengthening the bonds of the Christian community.

Fasting Through the Middle Ages: A Time of Spiritual Renewal

During the Middle Ages, fasting continued to be an important practice in Christian life. The Church established specific fasting periods, such as Lent, a forty-day fast leading up to Easter, and Advent, a time of preparation before Christmas. These periods of fasting were seen as times of spiritual renewal, repentance, and preparation for the celebration of important Christian events.

Fasting during this time was often accompanied by other forms of asceticism, such as prayer, almsgiving, and penance. The Church encouraged fasting as a way to draw closer to God, seek forgiveness for sins, and cultivate a spirit of humility and dependence on divine grace.

The Middle Ages also saw the rise of new monastic orders, such as the Franciscans and Dominicans, who continued the tradition of fasting as part of their spiritual discipline. These orders emphasized the importance of fasting as a way to live out the gospel, serve the poor, and follow the example of Christ.

The Reformation and Beyond: Fasting in the Modern Christian World

With the Reformation in the sixteenth century, the practice of fasting in the Christian Church began to change. Reformers such as Martin Luther and John Calvin criticized what they saw as the legalism and excesses of the medieval Church's fasting practices. While they did not reject fasting outright, they emphasized that fasting should be done with the right heart and attitude, not as a mere outward show of piety.

In the modern Christian world, fasting continues to be an important practice, though it is often approached in different ways by different denominations. Some Christians observe traditional fasting periods such as Lent, while others may fast on specific days or during times of personal or communal prayer. The emphasis today is often on the spiritual benefits of fasting, rather than the physical abstinence itself.

As we have seen, fasting is a practice that has been embraced by countless cultures and religions throughout history as a way to connect with the divine, purify the body and soul, and cultivate spiritual virtues.

In the chapters to come, we will explore how fasting is not only a spiritual discipline but also a scientifically proven practice that benefits our physical and mental health. As we delve deeper into the subject, we will see how the spiritual and scientific aspects of fasting are not opposed but complementary, each enhancing the other in ways that are both profound and transformative.

CHAPTER 2

THE CALL TO BIBLICAL FASTING

The Bible is our ultimate guide for living a life that pleases God. It reveals His heart, His will, and His ways. As Christians, we are called to align our lives with the teachings of Scripture, and fasting is one of the spiritual disciplines that God has given us to deepen our relationship with Him. From Genesis to Revelation, fasting appears as a consistent practice among God's people, a practice that reflects a heart fully surrendered to the Lord.

In this chapter, we will explore what the Bible says about fasting. We will examine the commands, examples, and teachings related to fasting, seeking to understand why fasting is so important and how to incorporate it into our spiritual lives. Whether you are new to fasting or have practiced it for years, my hope is that this chapter will deepen your understanding and inspire you to embrace fasting as a vital part of your walk with God.

SHOULD BELIEVERS FAST? A BIBLICAL MANDATE

One of the most common questions Christians ask is whether fasting is still relevant today. After all, we live under the New Covenant, where Christ has fulfilled the Law. So, should believers still fast?

The answer is a resounding yes. While fasting is not a legal requirement, it is a powerful and essential discipline for every believer. Jesus Himself assumed that His followers would fast. In Matthew 6:16-18 (NIV), during the Sermon on the Mount, Jesus said:

"When you fast, do not look somber as the hypocrites do, for they disfigure their faces to show others they are fasting. Truly I tell you, they have received their reward in full. But when you fast, put oil on your head and wash your face, so that it will not be obvious to others that you are fasting, but only to your Father, who is unseen; and your Father, who sees what is done in secret, will reward you."

Notice that Jesus did not say "if you fast," but "when you fast." This language suggests that fasting is expected of believers, just as prayer and generosity are expected. Jesus's words make it clear that fasting is not about outward appearances or religious performance; it is about seeking God with a sincere heart, desiring to draw closer to Him.

Additionally, in Matthew 9:15, Jesus responded to questions about why His disciples were not fasting by saying, "The time will come when the bridegroom will be taken from them; then they will fast" (NIV). Jesus was referring to Himself as the bridegroom, and His statement implies that after His ascension, His followers would indeed fast. As the Church awaits the return of Christ, fasting remains a practice that helps us to stay spiritually vigilant, humble, and connected to God.

FASTING IN THE OLD TESTAMENT: DRAWING NEAR TO GOD

The practice of fasting is deeply rooted in the Old Testament. It was a common practice among God's people, particularly during times of distress, repentance, and seeking divine intervention. Fasting was often associated with mourning, repentance, and a desire to draw closer to God.

One of the earliest mentions of fasting is found in Leviticus 16:29-31, where God commanded the Israelites to observe a fast on the Day of Atonement (Yom Kippur). This was a solemn day of repentance, and the people were to "afflict their souls," which traditionally included fasting, as they sought atonement for their sins. The Day of Atonement was a time of deep reflection, humility, and seeking God's mercy.

Throughout the Old Testament, fasting was a way for individuals and communities to humble themselves before God and seek His favor. In 2 Samuel 12:16, we see David fasting and praying for the life of his child. Although God's will was ultimately done, David's fast was an expression of his deep sorrow and his desire to plead with God.

In the book of Esther, we see an entire nation fasting. When the Jewish people were faced with the threat of annihilation, Queen Esther called for a three-day fast, saying:

> Go, gather together all the Jews who are in Susa, and fast for me. Do not eat or drink for three days, night or day. I and my attendants will fast as you do. When this is done, I will go to the king, even though it is against the law. And if I perish, I perish. —Esther 4:16 (NIV)

The result of this fast was a miraculous deliverance for the Jewish people, showing us the power of collective fasting and prayer.

These examples from the Old Testament reveal that fasting is a powerful tool for seeking God's intervention, expressing repentance, and drawing near to Him. Fasting was not just a ritual; it was a heartfelt response to God, a way of saying, "Lord, I need You more than I need food. I am desperate for Your presence, Your guidance, and Your deliverance."

FASTING IN THE NEW TESTAMENT: FOLLOWING THE EXAMPLE OF JESUS

Fasting did not end with the Old Testament. In the New Testament, we see fasting continue as a significant practice among the followers of Christ. Jesus Himself set the example for us by fasting for forty days and forty nights before beginning His public ministry (Matthew 4:1-2). During this time, He was tempted by Satan but overcame each temptation by relying on the Word of God.

Jesus's fast in the wilderness teaches us several important lessons. First, it shows us that fasting is a time of preparation. Before launching into His ministry, Jesus sought the Father in solitude and fasting, preparing His heart and mind for the work ahead. As followers of Christ, we, too, should consider fasting to prepare for significant decisions, ministry endeavors, or times of spiritual renewal.

Second, Jesus's fast demonstrates the power of God's Word in overcoming temptation. Even though Jesus was physically weak after forty days without food, He was spiritually strong, able to resist the devil's temptations by quoting Scripture. Fasting can help us to sharpen our spiritual focus, resist the enemy's attacks, and stand firm in the truth of God's Word.

The early Church continued the practice of fasting as they sought God's guidance and power. In Acts 13:2-3, we read that the church in Antioch was worshiping the Lord and fasting when the Holy Spirit directed them to set apart Barnabas and Saul for the work to which He had called them. After fasting and praying, they laid their hands on them and sent them off. This passage highlights how fasting was integral to discerning God's will and commissioning leaders for ministry.

Fasting was also a regular practice for the Apostle Paul. In 2 Corinthians 11:27, Paul mentions that he often fasted as part of his dedication to the ministry and his desire to walk closely with the Lord. Paul understood that fasting was not about earning favor with God, but about humbling himself and aligning his heart with God's purposes.

THE SPIRITUAL SIGNIFICANCE OF FASTING

Fasting, as seen throughout the Bible, is not merely an act of self-denial. It is a spiritual discipline that carries deep significance and purpose. When we fast, we are declaring that our need for God is greater than our need for physical sustenance. We are humbling ourselves before Him, acknowledging that we are not self-sufficient and that we depend on Him for everything.

One of the primary purposes of fasting is to seek God's presence and to deepen our relationship with Him. In Joel 2:12, God calls His people to "return to me with all your heart, with fasting and weeping and mourning" (NIV). Fasting is a way of expressing our wholehearted devotion to God—our way of saying, "Lord, I need You more than anything else in this world."

Fasting is also a way of expressing repentance and seeking God's forgiveness. In the book of Jonah, the people of Nineveh responded to Jonah's message of impending judgment with fasting and repentance.

The king of Nineveh proclaimed a fast for all the people, and they turned from their wicked ways. As a result, God had compassion on them and did not bring the destruction He had threatened (Jonah 3:5-10). This account shows us the power of fasting and repentance to move the heart of God and bring about His mercy.

Furthermore, fasting is a means of intercession, a way of standing in the gap for others and pleading with God on their behalf. In the book of Daniel, we see the prophet fasting and praying for the restoration of Jerusalem. Daniel's fast was a time of intense prayer and intercession, and it resulted in a powerful revelation from God (Daniel 9:3-23). When we fast and pray for others, we are engaging in spiritual warfare, contending for God's will to be done in their lives.

FASTING WITH THE RIGHT HEART: AVOIDING HYPOCRISY

While fasting is a powerful spiritual discipline, it is crucial that we approach it with the right heart. Throughout Scripture, we see warnings against fasting for the wrong reasons or with the wrong motives. In Isaiah 58, God rebukes the people of Israel for their hypocritical fasting. They were fasting to seek their own pleasure and oppress their workers rather than seeking God's heart and living out His commands. God declares, "Is not this the fast that I choose: to loose the bonds of wickedness, to undo the straps of the yoke, to let the oppressed go free, and to break every yoke?" (Isaiah 58:6, ESV)

Jesus also warned against fasting for the sake of appearances. In Matthew 6:16-18, He cautioned His disciples not to fast like the hypocrites who disfigure their faces to show others they are fasting. Instead, He taught that fasting should be done in secret, with a heart that seeks to please God rather than gain the approval of others.

Fasting, when done with the right heart, is a beautiful act of worship and devotion. It is an opportunity to humble ourselves, seek God's face, and align our hearts with His will. When we fast with the right motives, God promises to reward us (Matthew 6:18). The rewards of fasting are not just physical or material; they are spiritual and eternal. Through fasting, we can experience a deeper intimacy with God, greater spiritual strength, and a clearer sense of His direction in our lives.

As we conclude this chapter on biblical fasting, it is clear that fasting is not just an ancient practice, but a vital and relevant discipline for every believer today. The Bible teaches us that fasting is a powerful way to seek God's presence, express repentance, intercede for others, and prepare for His work in our lives.

Fasting is not about earning God's favor or manipulating Him to do our will. Rather, it is about humbling ourselves before Him, acknowledging our dependence on His grace, and aligning our hearts with His purposes. When we fast, we are saying, "Lord, I need You more than food, more than anything else. I want to know You more, love You more, and follow You more closely."

As you consider incorporating fasting into your spiritual life, I encourage you to approach it with a heart of sincerity, humility, and devotion. Let your fasting be an act of worship, a time of drawing near to God and seeking His face. And as you fast, remember the words of Jesus: "Your Father, who sees what is done in secret, will reward you" (Matthew 6:18, NIV).

May your times of fasting be filled with God's presence, power, and peace, and may they lead you into a deeper and more intimate relationship with your Heavenly Father.

CHAPTER 3

THE RELATIONSHIP BETWEEN PRAYER AND FASTING

Prayer and fasting are two of the most powerful spiritual disciplines in the Christian life. They are like two wings of a bird—each essential for lifting us into the heights of spiritual communion with God. While prayer connects us directly to the heart of God, fasting amplifies that connection, intensifying our focus, humility, and dependence on Him. When combined, prayer and fasting create a spiritual synergy that can break strongholds, bring divine breakthrough, and draw us into a deeper relationship with the Lord.

In this chapter, we will explore the intimate connection between prayer and fasting, understanding how these practices complement and strengthen each other. Through biblical examples of prayer and fasting, we can uncover the spiritual power that emerges when they are united and discover how to incorporate both disciplines into our daily walk with God. My prayer is that by the end of this chapter, you will be inspired to embrace prayer and fasting as a dynamic duo in your own spiritual journey.

THE FOUNDATION: PRAYER AS OUR LIFELINE TO GOD

Before we dive into the relationship between prayer and fasting, it's important to first understand the foundational role of prayer in the life of a believer. Prayer is our lifeline to God—it is the primary way we communicate with Him, express our needs, and align our hearts with His will. Through prayer, we come into His presence, lay our burdens at His feet, and listen for His voice.

The Bible portrays prayer as an essential part of our relationship with God. Jesus Himself modeled a life of prayer, often withdrawing to solitary places to pray (Luke 5:16). The apostles devoted themselves to prayer, understanding that it was through prayer that they could receive guidance, strength, and power from the Holy Spirit (Acts 1:14; Acts 6:4).

Prayer is more than just asking God for things—it is an act of worship, a way of drawing near to God and building intimacy with Him. It is through prayer that we experience His presence, receive His wisdom, and find peace in His promises. The apostle Paul exhorts us to "pray without ceasing" (1 Thessalonians 5:17, ESV), emphasizing the importance of maintaining a continual connection with God through prayer.

When we add fasting to our prayer life, we are taking our communion with God to another level. Fasting is like turning up the volume on our prayers, allowing us to hear God's voice more clearly and to pray with greater focus and fervency.

Fasting as an Intensifier of Prayer

Fasting, as we have discussed, is the voluntary abstention from food (or other physical needs) for a spiritual purpose. But fasting is not just about giving up food; it's about replacing that physical nourishment with spiritual nourishment. It's about turning away from the distractions of the world to focus more intently on God.

When we fast, we are telling our bodies that our spirit's hunger for God is greater than our physical hunger. We are declaring that we are willing to deny ourselves the comforts of this world to seek the eternal riches of God's presence. Fasting intensifies our prayers because it aligns our entire being—body, soul, and spirit—with the purposes of God.

In Joel 2:12-13, God calls His people to return to Him with all their hearts, with fasting, weeping, and mourning. This passage highlights the connection between fasting and heartfelt prayer. Fasting is a way of expressing the intensity of our prayers, showing God that we are serious about seeking Him and that we are willing to humble ourselves before Him.

The Bible provides numerous examples of how fasting intensifies prayer and leads to powerful spiritual breakthroughs. One of the most compelling examples is found in the book of Daniel. In Daniel 9, we read about how Daniel turned to the Lord in prayer and fasting, seeking God's mercy for the people of Israel. He prayed fervently, confessing the sins of his people and asking God to restore Jerusalem. In response to Daniel's prayer and fasting, God sent the angel Gabriel to give him insight and understanding, revealing the future of Israel and the coming of the Messiah (Daniel 9:20-27).

This example shows us that fasting can amplify our prayers, making them more powerful and effective. When we fast, we are not just praying with our words; we are praying with our entire being, bringing our bodies into submission to the will of God and demonstrating our deep desire for His intervention.

The Spiritual Power of Combined Prayer and Fasting

Prayer and fasting, when combined, have the power to break strongholds, bring deliverance, and open doors for divine intervention. This power is not because of any inherent virtue in fasting itself, but because fasting aligns us more closely with God's will, making our prayers more fervent, focused, and effective.

One of the most striking examples of the power of combined prayer and fasting is found in the story of Jehoshaphat, the king of Judah. In 2 Chronicles 20, we read that a vast army came against Judah, and Jehoshaphat was terrified. But instead of panicking, he called for a nationwide fast. The people of Judah came together to seek the Lord, and Jehoshaphat prayed, acknowledging their helplessness and asking God to deliver them. In response, God gave them a prophetic word of victory, and without even lifting a sword, the people of Judah watched as God caused their enemies to destroy each other (2 Chronicles 20:1-30).

This story teaches us that fasting and prayer are powerful weapons in spiritual warfare. When we humble ourselves through fasting and seek God's face in prayer, we invite His power into our situations, and He can do exceedingly abundantly above all that we ask or think (Ephesians 3:20).

In the Gospel of Mark, Jesus taught His disciples about the power of prayer and fasting in overcoming spiritual obstacles. After His disciples were unable to cast out a demon from a boy, Jesus explained that "this kind can come out by nothing but prayer and fasting" (Mark 9:29). This statement underscores the fact that some spiritual breakthroughs require more than just prayer—they require the added intensity and focus that fasting brings.

Practical Tips for Combining Prayer and Fasting

As we have seen, the combination of prayer and fasting is a powerful tool for deepening our relationship with God and experiencing His power in our lives. But how do we practically combine these disciplines in our daily walk?

1) **Set Clear Spiritual Goals:** Before you begin a fast, take time to pray and ask God what He wants to accomplish in your life through the fast. Whether it's a breakthrough in a specific area, guidance for a decision, or a deeper relationship with Him, having clear spiritual goals will help you stay focused during the fast.

2) **Schedule Regular Prayer Times:** During your fast, set aside specific times each day for prayer. These can be times of focused prayer, where you seek God's presence, pray through Scripture, and present your requests to Him. Let these times be moments of intimacy with God, where you pour out your heart to Him and listen for His voice.

3) **Use Scripture as a Foundation for Your Prayers:** Praying through Scripture during your fast can be incredibly powerful. Find verses that relate to your spiritual goals and pray them back to God, declaring His promises over your life. The Word of God is living and active (Hebrews 4:12), and when you pray according to His Word, you are aligning your prayers with His will.

4) **Incorporate Worship and Praise:** Fasting and prayer should not be burdensome; they should be filled with the joy of the Lord. Include times of worship and praise in your fast, thanking God for His goodness, His faithfulness, and His love. Worship

shifts your focus from your needs to God's greatness, and it invites His presence into your life.

5) **Journal Your Prayers and Insights:** Keep a journal during your fast where you can write down your prayers, insights, and any revelations you receive from God. Journaling helps you track your spiritual journey, and it can serve as a record of God's faithfulness that you can look back on in the future.

6) **Stay Physically Hydrated and Rested:** While fasting, it's important to take care of your physical body as well. Make sure you drink plenty of water and get enough rest. Physical hydration and rest will help you maintain your focus and energy during your times of prayer.

7) **Be Open to the Leading of the Holy Spirit:** As you fast and pray, be sensitive to the leading of the Holy Spirit. He may guide you to pray for specific people, situations, or issues that you hadn't considered before. Follow His promptings and trust that He is guiding you according to God's will.

As you embrace the practice of prayer and fasting, remember that it is not about earning God's favor or trying to manipulate Him into doing what you want. Rather, it is about humbling yourself before Him, seeking His face, and aligning your heart with His purposes. Through prayer and fasting, you can experience greater intimacy with God, deeper spiritual insight, and powerful breakthroughs that only He can bring.

I encourage you to make prayer and fasting a regular part of your spiritual life. Whether it's a short fast or an extended period of fasting and prayer, approach it with a heart of humility, dependence, and devotion. As you do, you will find that God is faithful to meet you, to strengthen you, and to lead you into the fullness of His plans and

The Relationship Between Prayer and Fasting

purposes for your life. May your journey of prayer and fasting be filled with God's presence, power, and peace, and may you experience the joy of walking closely with your Heavenly Father.

CHAPTER 4

FASTING PROFILES IN THE BIBLICAL NARRATIVE

Fasting is a spiritual discipline that God has woven into the fabric of His people's relationship with Him throughout the Bible. From the early days of Israel's formation to the establishment of the Church in the New Testament, fasting was not just a ritual; it was a powerful expression of repentance, intercession, and dependence on God. In this chapter, we will take a deep dive into the major fasts that God called His people to in the Old Testament, as well as those who fasted in the New Testament, tracing the lives of key individuals who fasted and the outcomes of their fasts. By the end of this chapter, you will gain a comprehensive understanding of what biblical fasting looked like and how it shaped the course of history for God's people.

FASTING IN THE OLD TESTAMENT: GOD'S CALL TO HIS PEOPLE

Throughout the Old Testament, God called the nation of Israel to fast during critical moments in their history. These fasts were often linked to times of national repentance, seeking God's mercy, and preparing for significant spiritual events. Let's explore some of the most notable fasts that God commanded His people to undertake.

1) The Day of Atonement (Yom Kippur): A National Fast of Repentance (Leviticus 16:29-31)

The most significant and enduring fast in the Old Testament is the Day of Atonement, known as Yom Kippur. This annual fast was instituted by God as a day of repentance and spiritual cleansing for the entire nation of Israel. Leviticus 16 details the instructions for Yom Kippur, where God commanded the Israelites to "afflict their souls" (Leviticus 16:29-31, ESV), which was understood to include fasting. On this day, the high priest would enter the Holy of Holies to make atonement for the sins of the people, and the Israelites were to fast, abstaining from food and humbling themselves before God.

Yom Kippur was a solemn day of introspection, repentance, and reconciliation with God. It was a time for the people of Israel to acknowledge their sins, seek God's forgiveness, and renew their covenant relationship with Him. The fast on Yom Kippur was a reminder that sin separates us from God, and that only through repentance and atonement can we be restored to fellowship with Him.

The significance of Yom Kippur extended beyond the physical act of fasting—it was a spiritual discipline that pointed to the ultimate atonement that would be made through Jesus Christ. As believers today, Yom Kippur serves as a powerful reminder of the seriousness of sin, the need for repentance, and the grace that we have received through Christ's sacrifice.

2) Fasting at Mount Sinai: Moses's Forty Days of Intercession (Deuteronomy 9:18)

Another major fast in the Old Testament occurred when Moses fasted for forty days and forty nights on Mount Sinai. This fast took place after the Israelites had sinned by worshiping the golden calf, breaking the covenant they had just made with God. In response, Moses ascended the mountain to intercede on behalf of the people, seeking God's forgiveness and pleading for His continued presence with them.

Deuteronomy 9:18 recounts Moses's fast: "Then I lay prostrate before the LORD as before, forty days and forty nights. I neither ate bread nor drank water, because of all the sin that you had committed, in doing what was evil in the sight of the LORD to provoke him to anger." Moses's fast was an act of deep intercession and repentance on behalf of the nation. Through his fasting and prayer, God relented from His anger, forgave the people, and renewed His covenant with them.

The outcome of Moses's fast was the reestablishment of the covenant, with God giving Moses a second set of tablets containing the Ten Commandments. This fast emphasizes the power of intercessory fasting and the importance of seeking God's forgiveness for ourselves and others. It also highlights the role of leaders in standing in the gap for their people, bringing their sins before God in humble repentance.

3) Israel's Corporate Fast at Mizpah: A Moment of Repentance and Victory (1 Samuel 7:5-6)

The Israelites gathered at Mizpah in a powerful scene of unity, fasting together under Samuel's leadership. This wasn't just about skipping meals—it was a cry for deliverance from the Philistines and a return to God after a season of idolatry. And God heard them! Their fast led to a miraculous victory, proving that when a community seeks God in humility, He steps in powerfully.

The corporate fast at Mizpah was a powerful act of repentance and renewal for Israel. Under oppression from the Philistines, the nation had drifted from God, plagued by idolatry and defeat. Recognizing the need for spiritual realignment, the prophet Samuel called the people to Mizpah, where they gathered to fast, repent, and seek God's intervention.

As they fasted, they symbolically poured out water before the Lord, representing their repentance and complete reliance on God. Together, they confessed their sins, humbling themselves before Him. While they fasted, the Philistines saw this gathering as a chance to attack, but Samuel cried out to God, and He responded mightily. Scripture tells us, "The LORD thundered with a loud thunder upon the Philistines.... they were overcome before Israel" (1 Samuel 7:10). God's intervention through a sudden thunderstorm scattered the Philistine forces, allowing Israel to pursue and defeat them.

This victory marked a spiritual turning point, and Israel experienced peace for years following. The fast at Mizpah is a timeless example of how sincere, united repentance and fasting can invite divine intervention and lead to breakthrough and lasting renewal for a nation.

4) King David's Fast for His Son: A Story of Sorrow and Surrender (2 Samuel 12:15-23)

David's fast for his gravely ill son is a profound example of fasting in times of crisis. After his sin with Bathsheba, David's child became critically ill, and in a heartfelt appeal to God, David fasted, abstaining from food and praying intensely for the child's healing. David's actions during this time reflected his deep sorrow and his hope that God might show mercy by sparing the child's life. He lay on the ground, refusing comfort from others, fully dedicating himself to seeking God's intervention.

Despite David's fervent fasting and prayers, the child ultimately passed away. Remarkably, David's response after receiving the news shows a deep acceptance of God's will. He ended his fast, bathed, and returned to the house of the Lord to worship. When questioned by his servants, David explained that while the child lived, there was hope God might relent. However, with the child's passing, he recognized God's judgment and chose to surrender fully to God's sovereignty. David's fast underscores that, while fasting can be a powerful means of seeking God, it ultimately aligns us with His will rather than changing His decrees.

5) Elijah's Forty-Day Fast: A Journey of Renewal and Revelation (1 Kings 19:4-8)

Elijah's forty-day fast came during a period of fear and exhaustion. After a great victory over the prophets of Baal, Elijah found himself fleeing from Queen Jezebel, who threatened his life. Alone and discouraged, he went into the wilderness, praying to God to take his life, feeling he could no longer continue. God responded not with rebuke but with supernatural provision, sending an angel to feed him. Twice, Elijah ate this divinely provided food, which miraculously sustained him for a forty-day journey to Mount Horeb.

At Horeb, Elijah's fast served as a time of spiritual renewal and alignment with God's will. It was there, in a quiet encounter, that God revealed Himself not through dramatic displays, but through a gentle whisper, speaking to Elijah's heart. Strengthened and refocused,

Elijah received instructions to anoint new leaders in Israel, which would ultimately fulfill God's plans for the nation. Elijah's fast illustrates how, in moments of exhaustion or despair, fasting can open us to God's comfort and guidance, providing the renewal needed to continue His work.

6) Ahab's Fast of Repentance: A Surprising Act of Humility (1 Kings 21:27-29)

King Ahab, known as one of Israel's most wicked rulers, performed an unexpected act of humility by fasting after the prophet Elijah confronted him about his grievous sins, especially his role in Naboth's murder to seize his vineyard. Struck by Elijah's words of judgment—that disaster would soon befall his household—Ahab responded by tearing his clothes, donning sackcloth, and fasting. This was not typical of Ahab, who often ignored God's commands, yet here he showed genuine remorse, humbling himself publicly.

God took note of Ahab's repentance. Though judgment was still inevitable due to Ahab's many sins, God honored Ahab's humility by delaying the impending punishment, allowing it to fall after Ahab's death rather than during his lifetime. Ahab's fast reminds us of the power of genuine repentance, even in the life of someone known for rebellion. His story shows that, regardless of past actions, humbling oneself before God can lead to mercy and a reprieve, underscoring that God values a heart that truly seeks forgiveness.

7) Fasting During National Crises: Jehoshaphat and the People of Judah (2 Chronicles 20:3-4)

In times of national crisis, God's people often turned to fasting as a means of seeking His intervention and deliverance. One of the most notable examples of this is found in the story of King Jehoshaphat. When Judah was threatened by a vast army of Moabites, Ammonites, and Meunites, Jehoshaphat was filled with fear. However, instead of succumbing to panic, he proclaimed a fast for all of Judah.

In 2 Chronicles 20:3-4 (ESV), we read, "Jehoshaphat was afraid and set his face to seek the LORD, and proclaimed a fast throughout all Judah. And Judah assembled to seek help from the LORD; from all the cities of Judah they came to seek the LORD." The entire nation gathered to fast and pray, seeking God's guidance and protection.

God responded to their fasting and prayer by speaking through the prophet Jahaziel, who assured them of victory without having to fight. The next day, as the people of Judah went out to face the enemy, they began to sing and praise the Lord, and God caused their enemies to turn on each other, leading to a miraculous victory for Judah.

This fast demonstrates the power of corporate fasting and prayer in times of crisis. It shows that when God's people humble themselves, seek His face, and trust in His power, He is faithful to deliver them. The story of Jehoshaphat and the people of Judah is a testament to the fact that fasting can lead to divine intervention and victory in the face of overwhelming odds.

8) Ezra's Fast for Protection: Seeking God's Guidance for the Journey (Ezra 8:21-23)

Ezra led the Jewish exiles in a fast as they prepared to return to Jerusalem, a journey filled with potential dangers. Rather than asking the Persian king for military protection, Ezra chose to rely solely on God, proclaiming a communal fast by the Ahava Canal. This fast was a powerful display of faith, as Ezra and the people sought God's protection and guidance for their journey home, demonstrating their trust in Him over any human assistance.

The fast lasted one day, during which the entire community humbled themselves, praying and seeking God's favor. Their purpose was clear—to ask for divine protection against the threats of robbers and ambushes on the long journey ahead. God honored their act of faith, and as a result, they safely arrived in Jerusalem, carrying valuable offerings for the Temple without incident. Ezra's fast highlights how fasting and prayer can serve as a means to seek God's guidance and protection, especially when we commit fully to trusting Him for our safety and provision.

9) Nehemiah's Fast for Jerusalem: A Call to Rebuild (Nehemiah 1:4)

When Nehemiah, a Jewish exile serving in Persia, received news that Jerusalem's walls lay in ruins, he was devastated. This wasn't just about broken walls; it was a symbol of the vulnerability and shame of God's people. In response, Nehemiah entered a period of intense fasting and prayer, seeking God's guidance and favor for a way to help restore the city.

Though the exact duration of Nehemiah's fast isn't specified, his prayer was heartfelt and specific—he confessed Israel's sins, reminded God of His promises, and asked for favor before the king. Nehemiah's fasting was an act of humility and dependence, showing his total reliance on God to intervene. In a remarkable outcome, God answered. King Artaxerxes not only granted Nehemiah permission to return to Jerusalem but also provided resources and protection to support the rebuilding effort. Nehemiah's fast exemplifies how fasting can align us with God's purposes and open doors of opportunity, even in seemingly impossible circumstances.

10) Fasting for Deliverance: The Story of Esther (Esther 4:16)
The book of Esther provides another powerful example of fasting during a time of national crisis. When the Jewish people were threatened with annihilation by the wicked plot of Haman, Esther, the queen of Persia, called for a three-day fast. She asked all the Jews in Susa to join her in fasting and prayer as she prepared to approach the king—a move that could have cost her life.

In Esther 4:16 (ESV), she said, "Go, gather all the Jews to be found in Susa, and hold a fast on my behalf, and do not eat or drink for three days, night or day. I and my young women will also fast as you do. Then I will go to the king, though it is against the law, and if I perish, I perish." This fast was an act of deep humility and dependence on God, as the Jewish people sought His intervention to save them from destruction.

The outcome of this fast was nothing short of miraculous. God turned the heart of the king, exposed Haman's wicked plot, and brought about a great deliverance for His people. The story of Esther's fast teaches us that fasting can be a powerful tool for seeking God's deliverance in times of crisis. When we face situations that seem impossible, fasting helps us focus our prayers, seek God's intervention, and trust in His sovereignty.

11) Daniel's Fasts: Faithfulness and Revelation (Daniel 1:8-16; 10:1-3)
Daniel's commitment to fasting is seen in two distinct instances, each with unique purposes and outcomes. The first fast occurred when

Daniel and his friends were brought to Babylon and faced the king's rich food, which could compromise their spiritual purity. Daniel proposed a ten-day partial fast, where they ate only vegetables and drank water. By the end of this fast, Daniel and his friends appeared healthier than the others, gaining favor and positions of influence in the Babylonian court.

In the second instance, Daniel embarked on a twenty-one-day partial fast, abstaining from meat, wine, and rich foods, as he sought God's guidance and understanding concerning Israel's future. The outcomes of Daniel's fasts reveal just how powerful this spiritual discipline can be when approached with humility and faith.

- **Physical Health and Favor:** After the initial ten-day fast, Daniel and his friends appeared healthier and stronger than those who consumed the king's rich food. This visible difference granted them favor in the eyes of their overseers and reinforced their conviction that God was with them.
- **Increased Wisdom:** God rewarded Daniel's faithfulness by granting him wisdom, knowledge, and the supernatural ability to interpret dreams. This set him apart in the Babylonian court, leading to opportunities and influence that would otherwise have been inaccessible.
- **Spiritual Breakthrough and Angelic Encounter:** In response to his twenty-one-day fast, Daniel received an angelic visitation. The angel revealed that from the very first day that Daniel had set his heart to fast and pray, God had heard his prayers. However, there had been spiritual resistance delaying the angel's arrival, illustrating how Daniel's fasting played a role in overcoming unseen obstacles.

Daniel's fast teaches us that fasting is more than abstaining from food; it is an intentional posture of the heart. His example shows that when we humble ourselves and prioritize God, He meets us with favor, wisdom, and revelation. Daniel's story reminds us that fasting can lead to both physical vitality and spiritual breakthrough. For modern believers, Daniel's fast serves as a powerful model, inspiring us to seek God with a heart of devotion and to embrace fasting as a transformative discipline in our own lives.

12) Joel's Call to Corporate Fasting: A Cry for Mercy (Joel 1:14; 2:12-17)

In the book of Joel, the prophet calls the people of Israel to a communal fast during a devastating crisis. The land had been ravaged by a locust plague and drought, leaving the people in despair and desperate for relief. Joel urged the nation to gather, fast, and turn back to God with sincere repentance, saying, "Turn to Me with all your heart, with fasting, with weeping, and with mourning" (Joel 2:12). This fast was a collective cry for God's mercy and a plea for deliverance.

Joel's call wasn't simply about averting disaster; it was about restoring the people's relationship with God. By fasting, they demonstrated humility and sought to realign their lives with God's will. Although the outcome isn't described in detail, Joel's message underscored that genuine repentance could bring God's mercy, leading to healing and restoration for the land. This call to fasting highlights how communal repentance can be a powerful response in times of crisis, inviting God's favor and renewing hope for the future.

13) The Israelites' Fasts in Times of Crisis and War: Seeking God's Favor (Judges 20:26; Samuel 1:12)

Throughout Israel's history, fasting was a communal response to moments of crisis, loss, or defeat. In Judges 20, after a brutal defeat in battle, the Israelites gathered to fast, weep, and seek God's guidance. They humbled themselves, recognizing their need for God's favor and direction before continuing their struggle. Similarly, in 2 Samuel 1, the Israelites mourned and fasted following the death of King Saul and his son Jonathan. This fast served as a public expression of their grief and respect, while also preparing them for the leadership transitions ahead.

These fasts were acts of humility and reflection, allowing the people to turn to God in their despair and seek His wisdom and intervention. Although the immediate outcomes varied, each fast emphasized the importance of seeking God's favor and aligning with His will in times of adversity, reminding Israel to rely on God for guidance and strength in difficult circumstances.

CHAPTER 5

FASTING IN THE NEW TESTAMENT: JESUS AND THE EARLY CHURCH

Fasting was not confined to the Old Testament—it continued to be a vital spiritual discipline in the New Testament, with Jesus Himself setting the ultimate example. In the New Testament, we see key figures who fasted as they sought to align themselves with God's will and prepare for significant spiritual tasks.

1) Jesus's Forty-Day Fast: Preparation for Ministry (Matthew 4:1-2)

Jesus's fast in the wilderness is one of the most significant fasts recorded in the New Testament. Before beginning His public ministry, Jesus was led by the Spirit into the wilderness, where He fasted for forty days and forty nights. During this time, He was tempted by Satan, but He resisted each temptation by relying on the Word of God. Matthew 4:1-2 (ESV) tells us, "Then Jesus was led up by the Spirit into the wilderness to be tempted by the devil. And after fasting forty days and forty nights, he was hungry." Jesus's fast was a time of preparation, spiritual empowerment, and victory over the enemy. It teaches us that fasting can be a powerful tool for spiritual warfare, helping us to resist temptation and overcome the challenges that come our way.

The outcome of Jesus's fast was the beginning of His public ministry, marked by the power of the Holy Spirit. He emerged from the wilderness ready to preach the gospel, heal the sick, cast out demons, and ultimately fulfill His mission to redeem humanity. Jesus's example shows us that fasting is an essential part of preparing for ministry and fulfilling God's calling on our lives.

2) The Fast of Anna the Prophetess: A Life of Devotion (Luke 2:36-38)

Anna, an elderly prophetess, exemplified a life of devotion through regular fasting and prayer. Widowed early in life, she chose to dedicate herself entirely to God, spending her days and nights in the temple, fasting and praying. For Anna, fasting was more than a discipline; it was a lifestyle, an unbroken commitment to worship as she awaited the coming Messiah.

Anna's fasts were an expression of profound devotion. Her consistent worship and fasting underscored her faith, patience, and expectation, as she awaited God's promise of a Savior for Israel. As an outcome, Anna's faithfulness was rewarded when she encountered Jesus as an infant during His presentation at the temple. Recognizing Him as the promised Messiah, she praised God and shared the news with others who were also waiting for redemption. Anna's life of fasting positioned her to receive this revelation, a powerful testimony of how a life of dedication can lead to divine encounters.

3) The Disciples' Fast While Awaiting the Bridegroom: Fasting in Jesus's Absence (Matthew 9:14-15)

When questioned about why His disciples did not fast like other religious groups, Jesus responded that they would fast when He, the "Bridegroom," was taken away from them. While Jesus was with them, fasting was unnecessary because His presence fulfilled them. However, He foresaw a time after His departure when they would need to fast as a means of staying spiritually connected to Him.

Jesus indicated that fasting would become a way for His disciples to draw close to God in His physical absence, creating space for spiritual intimacy and dependence on God as they continued His work.

This statement established fasting as an integral practice for the early church, providing a foundation for deepening spiritual devotion. Following Jesus's ascension, His disciples indeed fasted regularly, using this discipline to seek guidance, strengthen their faith, and maintain their connection to God's presence.

4) The Church's Fast in Antioch: Commissioning for Mission (Acts 13:2-3)

The fast observed by the church leaders in Antioch stands as a powerful example of communal fasting for divine guidance. Gathered in a time of worship, prayer, and fasting, the leaders of the early church—including prophets and teachers—were seeking God's direction for their mission. At this pivotal moment, they set aside their own plans and concerns, focusing instead on discerning God's will for the spread of the gospel.

This fast was not driven by crisis or need, but by a desire to hear from the Holy Spirit regarding the church's next steps in ministry. The leaders were already active in teaching and spreading the gospel locally, but they sensed that God had a broader purpose for them. Their fasting and worship reflected a unified commitment to follow God's guidance as a community, demonstrating a proactive approach to ministry.

In response to their fasting and prayer, the Holy Spirit spoke clearly, instructing them to set apart Barnabas and Saul (later known as Paul) for missionary work. This divine direction marked the beginning of the first formal missionary journey, where Barnabas and Paul were commissioned to carry the gospel to the Gentile world. This fast led to one of the most significant expansions of Christianity, resulting in the establishment of churches across Asia Minor and the Mediterranean. Through their obedience in fasting, the Antioch church became a launching point for the global spread of the gospel, showing how fasting can bring clarity and purpose in fulfilling God's call.

5) Paul and Barnabas' Fast to Appoint Elders: A Dedication to God's Leadership (Acts 14:23)

As Paul and Barnabas concluded their missionary journey, they faced the critical task of appointing elders to lead the newly established churches. Recognizing the importance of solid, spiritually guided leadership, they engaged in a communal fast with each congregation, seeking God's guidance and blessing as they selected individuals to serve in these crucial roles.

This fast was an intentional time of dedication, where Paul and Barnabas sought God's wisdom and affirmation for those chosen to lead. Their approach to fasting underscores their reliance on God, demonstrating that leadership in the early church was not based on human preference but on spiritual discernment. Fasting here symbolized a commitment to entrust these leaders—and the congregations—to God's care.

Through fasting and prayer, Paul and Barnabas established a strong foundation for the new churches, ensuring that each community had leaders equipped to guide with integrity and spiritual authority. This practice of fasting for ordination not only affirmed God's hand in the leadership selection but also unified the congregations under a shared sense of purpose and devotion. By embedding fasting into the process, Paul and Barnabas helped create a model of leadership dedication that strengthened the early church and underscored the importance of God-centered authority.

6) Paul's Fast Following His Conversion: A Time of Transformation and Surrender (Acts 9:9)

After encountering Jesus on the road to Damascus, Paul was left physically blind and profoundly shaken. This experience marked a pivotal moment, transforming him from a persecutor of Christians to a follower of Christ. For the next three days, Paul fasted completely—without food or water—as he waited in Damascus, processing the radical encounter and seeking clarity on his future. This fast was Paul's first act of surrender, a symbolic cleansing as he turned from his past and prepared for a new path.

Paul's three-day fast was a profound period of repentance and openness to God's direction. He had been dramatically confronted by the truth of Christ, and fasting allowed him to fully focus on this divine revelation, dedicating his heart to understanding his new calling.

God responded by sending Ananias, a disciple, to restore Paul's sight and affirm his calling to preach the gospel. This fast marked Paul's official transformation from Saul, the persecutor, to Paul, the apostle. It was a time of spiritual preparation, paving the way for Paul's future ministry. His fast shows how surrendering through fasting can clear the way for God's purpose, marking the beginning of a life dedicated to service and evangelism.

7) Cornelius's Fast Before Receiving Peter: Opening the Door to the Gentiles (Acts 10:30-31)

Cornelius, a Roman centurion known for his devout faith, engaged in a period of fasting and prayer as he sought a deeper relationship with God. Although he was a Gentile, Cornelius lived a life of reverence, praying continually and giving generously to those in need. His fasting demonstrated a desire to know God more fully and receive guidance, not just for himself, but for his household as well.

Cornelius fasted with an open heart, seeking spiritual direction and expressing his devotion to God. His fast represented a deep hunger for truth, showing his dedication to pursuing God's will despite being outside the Jewish faith.

During this time of fasting, Cornelius received a divine vision instructing him to send for Peter, who would share the message of Christ with him and his household. This pivotal encounter marked the first time the gospel was formally presented to Gentiles, leading to the outpouring of the Holy Spirit upon Cornelius and his family. Cornelius's fast thus became a gateway through which the early church recognized that the gospel was for all people, expanding the reach of Christianity beyond Jewish believers and embracing a global mission.

8) The Fast of the Pharisees: A Lesson in True Devotion (Luke 18:12)

The Pharisees practiced a disciplined regimen of fasting twice a week as a mark of religious observance. This regular fasting, however, was often rooted more in pride and self-righteousness than in true humility or devotion to God. In the parable of the Pharisee and the tax collector, Jesus highlighted this attitude, as the Pharisee openly boasted about his fasting practices, contrasting his own "righteousness" with others he deemed less holy.

The Pharisees' fasting was intended to display piety and adherence to religious law, but in many cases, it became a means of promoting self-righteousness. Their focus was on outward appearances rather than a sincere, inward connection with God.

Jesus criticized this form of fasting, pointing out that genuine fasting should come from a place of humility and devotion. By highlighting the Pharisees' attitude, Jesus taught that fasting, to be meaningful, must be motivated by a true desire for God, not by a desire for public recognition or spiritual superiority. This lesson serves as a reminder that fasting is powerful only when it aligns with a humble, sincere heart.

The outcomes of fasting in the Bible were often dramatic and life changing. Whether it was the deliverance of the Jewish people in Esther's time, the rebuilding of Jerusalem under Nehemiah, or the establishment of the early Church, fasting played a crucial role in God's redemptive work throughout history. The results of fasting are not just limited to the immediate outcomes—often, the greatest results of fasting are the internal changes that take place in our hearts. Fasting helps us to grow in our dependence on God, deepen our relationship with Him, and be transformed into the likeness of Christ.

As we conclude this chapter, it is clear that fasting is a powerful and transformative spiritual discipline that has been integral to the life of God's people throughout the Bible. From the major fasts God called His people to in the Old Testament, to the key figures who fasted in the New Testament, fasting has played a crucial role in shaping the course of history for God's people. As you consider incorporating fasting into your spiritual life, I encourage you to learn from the examples of Moses, Esther, Nehemiah, Jesus, and the early Church. Let their stories inspire you to seek God with greater intensity, to trust in His power, and to experience the incredible results that come from fasting and prayer. May your times of fasting be filled with God's presence, power, and peace, and may you experience the joy of walking closely with your Heavenly Father as you follow the example of the saints who have gone before you.

CHAPTER 6

THE POWER OF CORPORATE FASTING

Fasting is often regarded as a deeply personal spiritual discipline, a time for individual believers to humble themselves before God, seek His face, and draw closer to Him. However, the Bible reveals another dimension of fasting that is equally powerful: corporate fasting. When God's people come together in unity to fast and pray, the spiritual impact can be transformative, not just for the individuals involved, but for entire communities, churches, and even nations.

In this chapter, we will explore the significance of corporate fasting in the Bible, from the Old Testament to the New Testament. We will examine the benefits of fasting as a church or community, and we will outline practical steps for organizing and participating in corporate fasts. As we delve into the Scriptures, we will discover how God honors the collective humility and seeking of His people, often responding with divine intervention, guidance, and revival.

CORPORATE FASTING IN THE OLD TESTAMENT: A PATTERN OF COMMUNAL SEEKING

The Old Testament provides numerous examples of corporate fasting, where entire communities or nations came together to seek God's intervention during times of crisis, repentance, or spiritual need. These examples illustrate the power of united fasting and prayer in moving the heart of God. The table below provides a summary of the corporate fasts that were undertaken in the Bible.

CORPORATE FAST	SCRIPTURE REFERENCE	PURPOSE OF THE FAST	DURATION OF THE FAST
JEHOSHAPHAT'S FAST	2 Chronicles 20:3-4	Seeking God's intervention and deliverance from a vast enemy army.	One day
NINEVEH'S FAST	Jonah 3:5-10	Repentance to avert God's impending judgment on the city.	Three days
EZRA'S FAST	Ezra 8:21-23	Seeking a safe journey for the exiles returning to Jerusalem.	One day
NEHEMIAH'S FAST	Nehemiah 9:1-3	Confession of sins and national repentance after the rebuilding of Jerusalem's walls.	Likely one day
ESTHER'S FAST	Esther 4:16	Seeking deliverance for the Jewish people from Haman's decree of genocide.	Three days
THE DAY OF ATONEMENT	Leviticus 23:26-32	Annual national repentance and atonement for the sins of Israel.	One day
SAMUEL'S FAST AT MIZPAH	1 Samuel 7:5-6	Repentance and seeking deliverance from the Philistines.	One day

CORPORATE FAST	SCRIPTURE REFERENCE	PURPOSE OF THE FAST	DURATION OF THE FAST
JOEL'S CALL TO FASTING	Joel 1:14; 2:12-17	Calling Israel to repentance and fasting in response to a severe locust plague and spiritual awakening.	Unknown
CORPORATE FAST IN ACTS	Acts 13:2-3	Seeking God's guidance for missionary commissioning (Paul and Barnabas).	Likely one day
FASTING IN ANTIOCH	Acts 14:23	Ordaining elders in new churches, seeking God's blessing and direction.	Unknown

BENEFITS OF CORPORATE FASTING: STRENGTH IN UNITY

Corporate fasting is more than just a group of individuals fasting together; it is a powerful expression of unity, humility, and collective seeking of God's will. When a church or community engages in corporate fasting, several significant benefits emerge.

1) **Spiritual Renewal and Revival**

One of the most profound benefits of corporate fasting is the spiritual renewal and revival that often follows. When God's people come together in humility and repentance, seeking His face through fasting and prayer, it creates an atmosphere ripe for the Holy Spirit to move powerfully.

Throughout church history, many revivals and spiritual awakenings have been preceded by corporate fasting and prayer. These seasons of seeking God together often lead to a deep conviction of sin, renewed passion for God's Word, and an outpouring of the Holy Spirit. Corporate fasting has the potential to ignite a fire of revival in the hearts of believers, transforming not only individuals but entire congregations and communities.

2) Increased Spiritual Unity

Corporate fasting fosters a deep sense of spiritual unity among believers. As the Apostle Paul writes in Ephesians 4:3, we are to be "endeavoring to keep the unity of the Spirit in the bond of peace." When a church or community commits to fasting together, it strengthens the bond of unity, as everyone is focused on the same spiritual goals and seeking God with one heart and mind.

This unity is not just an outward show of togetherness; it is a powerful spiritual reality that can break down barriers, heal divisions, and bring about a deeper sense of community within the Body of Christ. Jesus Himself prayed for unity among His followers (John 17:21), and corporate fasting is one way we can actively pursue and cultivate that unity.

3) Collective Breakthrough and Divine Intervention

As we have seen in the biblical examples, corporate fasting often leads to collective breakthrough and divine intervention. Whether it is deliverance from a national crisis, protection on a dangerous journey, or the sparing of a city from judgment, when God's people come together to fast and pray, He responds in powerful ways.

In today's world, corporate fasting can still lead to breakthrough in various areas—whether it's seeking God's direction for a church, interceding for a community in crisis, or standing in the gap for a nation. When believers unite in fasting, they tap into a spiritual power that is greater than the sum of its parts, inviting God to move in ways that might not happen through individual fasting alone.

Practical Steps for Organizing and Participating in Corporate Fasts

Given the profound significance and benefits of corporate fasting, how can a church or community effectively organize and participate in such a fast? Here are some practical steps to help guide the process.

1) **Clearly define the purpose of the fast**

Before embarking on a corporate fast, it is essential to clearly define the purpose of the fast. Is the church seeking God's direction for a specific decision? Is the community interceding for a particular need or crisis? Or is the focus on spiritual renewal and revival?

Having a clear purpose helps to unify the participants and ensures that everyone is fasting and praying with a common goal. It also provides direction for the prayers and activities that will take place during the fast.

2) **Communicate and prepare the congregation**

Once the purpose of the fast is established, it is important to communicate it clearly to the congregation or community. Leaders should provide ample notice and explanation, allowing time for individuals to prepare both spiritually and physically.

Preparation might include teachings or sermons on the biblical basis for fasting, practical advice on how to fast, and encouragement to seek God's guidance on how each person should participate. It is also helpful to provide resources such as prayer guides, Scripture readings, and fasting tips to support participants throughout the fast.

3) **Encourage different levels of participation**

Not everyone in a church or community may be able to fast in the same way. Some individuals may be able to participate in a full fast (abstaining from all food), while others may opt for a partial fast (abstaining from certain foods or meals). Some may choose to fast from non-food items, such as media or entertainment.

Encouraging different levels of participation ensures that everyone can take part in the fast according to their ability and conviction. The focus should be on the heart attitude behind the fast—humility, repentance, and seeking God—rather than on the specifics of what a person is fasting from.

4) **Provide opportunities for corporate prayer and worship**

During the fast, it is important to create opportunities for the church or community to come together for corporate prayer and worship. This could include special prayer meetings, worship services, or times of communal Scripture reading and meditation.

These gatherings help to reinforce the unity and purpose of the fast, allowing participants to encourage one another, share what God is speaking to them, and pray together for the needs and goals of the fast. Corporate worship during a fast can also be a powerful experience, as it brings the community into the presence of God with one voice and one heart.

5) **Conclude the fast with thanksgiving and celebration**

When the fast comes to an end, it is important to conclude it with a time of thanksgiving and celebration. This could be a special service or gathering where the church or community comes together to thank God for His faithfulness, share testimonies of what He has done during the fast, and celebrate the spiritual victories and breakthroughs that have been achieved.

This time of celebration helps to solidify the spiritual gains made during the fast and reinforces the sense of unity and community that has been built. It also serves as a reminder that fasting is not just about the abstention from food but about the spiritual feast we experience in God's presence.

Corporate fasting is a powerful and transformative practice that has been used by God's people throughout history to seek His face, align with His will, and invite His intervention in their lives. Whether it is for spiritual renewal, unity, or collective breakthrough, when believers come together to fast and pray, they tap into a deep well of spiritual power that can bring about profound change.

As you ponder organizing or participating in a corporate fast, remember the examples of Jehoshaphat, the people of Nineveh, Ezra, and the early Church. Let their stories inspire you to seek God with your community, to humble yourselves together before the Lord, and to experience the incredible power and presence of God that is released when His people fast and pray in unity.

May your corporate fasts be filled with the power and presence of God, and may they lead to lasting spiritual renewal, unity, and transformation in your church or community. And as you fast together, may you experience the joy of seeking God's face with one heart, one mind, and one voice.

CHAPTER 7

PREPARING FOR YOUR FAST

THE FOUNDATION OF A FRUITFUL FAST

While fasting is a powerful spiritual discipline, its effectiveness is often determined by how well we prepare for it. Just as a successful journey requires careful planning and preparation, so does a successful fast. The process of preparing for a fast involves more than just deciding to abstain from food—it requires setting clear spiritual goals, adopting the right mindset, and eliminating distractions that could hinder our focus on God.

In this chapter, we will explore how to prepare for your fast in a way that maximizes its spiritual impact. We will discuss the importance of setting specific spiritual goals, creating a fasting plan, cultivating the right mindset, and eliminating distractions so that you can fully engage with God during your fast. By the end of this chapter, you will have a comprehensive understanding of how to lay the groundwork for a successful and transformative fasting experience.

Setting Spiritual Goals and Creating a Fasting Plan

The first step in preparing for your fast is to set clear spiritual goals. Fasting without a purpose can lead to frustration and a sense of aimlessness. By defining what you hope to achieve spiritually through your fast, you can stay focused and motivated throughout the process.

1) **Identifying your Spiritual Goals**

When setting spiritual goals for your fast, consider what areas of your life you want to bring before God. These goals can be related to personal growth, relationships, ministry, or specific challenges you are facing. Here are some examples of spiritual goals you might consider:

- **Deepening your relationship with God:** Use your fast as a time to draw closer to God, seeking His presence and guidance in your life. This could involve spending more time in prayer, worship, and Scripture reading.
- **Seeking God's direction:** If you are facing a major decision or crossroads in your life, fasting can be a way to seek God's wisdom and direction. Ask God to reveal His will and give you clarity in your decision-making.
- **Interceding for others:** Fasting can be a powerful tool for intercessory prayer. You might choose to fast on behalf of a loved one, your church, or your community, asking God to intervene in specific situations or bring about spiritual breakthrough.
- **Overcoming personal struggles:** If you are battling sin, addiction, or any form of bondage, fasting can be a way to seek God's deliverance and strength. Use your fast as a time to repent, seek God's forgiveness, and ask for His power to overcome.
- **Spiritual renewal:** Perhaps you feel spiritually dry or disconnected from God. Fasting can be a way to rekindle your passion for the Lord, renew your commitment to Him, and experience spiritual revival.

Once you have identified your spiritual goals, write them down. Having your goals in writing will help you stay focused during your fast and remind you of why you are fasting when the going gets tough.

2) **Creating a Fasting Plan**

With your spiritual goals in place, the next step is to create a practical fasting plan. This plan should outline the specifics of how you will fast, including the type of fast you will undertake, the duration of the fast, and how you will structure your time during the fast.

Types of Fasts

Understanding the different types of fasts can be incredibly helpful for anyone embarking on a spiritual journey of fasting. Each type serves a unique purpose and offers flexibility, allowing individuals to choose a fast that aligns with their personal, physical, and spiritual needs. In this section, we'll explore several types of fasts mentioned in Scripture and practiced in the modern world. From the intensity of a complete fast to the structure of an intermittent fast, these variations provide a broad spectrum of ways to approach fasting, helping believers find a rhythm that supports both sustainability and spiritual depth. Whether you're new to fasting or seeking a deeper connection with God, these types of fasts offer practical insights to guide your journey.

- **Complete fast:** A complete fast involves abstaining from all food and consuming only water. This type of fast is typically undertaken for a shorter duration due to its intensity.
- **Partial fast:** A partial fast may involve abstaining from certain types of food, such as meat, sweets, or certain meals (e.g., fasting from sunrise to sunset). This type of fast is often more sustainable over a longer period.

- **Daniel fast:** Based on the fasting practices of Daniel in the Bible, this fast involves abstaining from rich foods like meat, sweets, and alcohol, and consuming only fruits, vegetables, and water.
- **Intermittent fast:** Intermittent fasting involves fasting for a certain number of hours each day (e.g., fasting for sixteen hours and eating during an eight-hour window). This can be a more flexible approach to fasting.

Duration and Themes of the Fast

The duration of a fast often reflects the depth of intention and the specific purpose behind it. Different durations allow believers to align their fast with a particular need, goal, or season in life, providing flexibility while drawing from biblical examples. From a single day of focused prayer to the transformative commitment of a forty-day fast, each timeframe offers unique opportunities for spiritual growth, renewal, and breakthrough. In this section, we'll explore various fasting durations and the themes they commonly represent. Whether you're seeking guidance, preparing for a new chapter, or simply longing for a closer walk with God, understanding the significance of each fasting duration can help you approach your fast with purpose and clarity.

- **One-day fast:** A one-day fast can be a powerful way to set aside time for focused prayer and seeking God. It is often used for specific prayer needs or as a regular spiritual discipline.
- **Three-day fast:** A three-day fast is commonly undertaken for deeper spiritual breakthroughs or to seek God's guidance in important matters.

- **Seven-day fast:** A seven-day fast allows for extended time in God's presence and can lead to significant spiritual renewal and clarity.
- **Ten-day fast:** From the example of Daniel and his kinsmen, this fast works best for body and mind by choosing to abstain from certain types of food leading to a rejuvenated body.
- **Fourteen-day fast:** A fourteen-day fast allows for deeper insight and clarity, both in the physical body as well as the depth of exploration in God.
- **Twenty-one-day fast:** Based on the example of Daniel, a twenty-one-day fast is often used for seeking God's direction, breaking spiritual strongholds, or engaging in extended intercessory prayer.
- **Forty-day fast:** A forty-day fast is modeled after Jesus's fast in the wilderness. It is a time of deep spiritual seeking, often undertaken for major life decisions, ministry preparation, or personal transformation.

Structuring Your Time

- **Prayer:** Schedule specific times for prayer throughout the day. This could include morning devotionals, midday prayers, and evening reflection. Use these times to bring your spiritual goals before God and seek His guidance and presence.
- **Scripture reading:** Choose a Bible reading plan or specific passages that align with your spiritual goals. Spend time meditating on God's Word and allowing it to speak into your life.
- **Journaling:** Keep a journal during your fast to record your prayers, insights, and what God is revealing to you. This will

help you track your spiritual journey and reflect on how God is moving in your life.
- **Worship:** Incorporate times of worship into your fast. Worship helps to shift your focus from your physical hunger to your spiritual hunger for God. Play worship music, sing, and praise God as you seek His face.

By creating a detailed fasting plan, you set yourself up for a successful fast. Your plan acts as a roadmap, guiding you through each day of the fast and helping you stay on track with your spiritual goals.

The Importance of Mindset in a Successful Fast

The success of your fast is not just about what you do externally; it's also about the mindset you bring into it. Your mindset can determine whether your fast becomes a time of spiritual breakthrough or just a period of physical deprivation. Here are key aspects of the mindset needed for a successful fast.

1) **Approach Your Fast with Expectancy**

As you begin your fast, approach it with a mindset of expectancy—believing that God will meet you in a powerful way. Fasting is not just a ritual; it is a spiritual journey where you encounter God in deeper and more intimate ways. Expect God to speak to you, to reveal His will, and to move in the areas you are fasting for.

Hebrews 11:6 reminds us, "But without faith *it is* impossible to please *Him*, for he who comes to God must believe that He is, and *that* He is a rewarder of those who diligently seek Him." As you fast, believe that God will reward your diligent seeking with His presence, guidance, and blessings.

2) **Cultivate a Heart of Humility**

Fasting is an act of humility before God. It is a way of acknowledging our dependence on Him and our need for His grace. As you fast, cultivate a heart of humility, recognizing that fasting is not about earning God's favor, but about positioning yourself to receive from Him.

James 4:10 says, "Humble yourselves in the sight of the Lord, and He will lift you up." As you humble yourself through fasting, trust that God will lift you up, renew your strength, and draw you closer to Him.

3) **Focus on the Spiritual, Not the Physical**

While fasting involves physical abstention from food or other comforts, the focus should be on the spiritual benefits rather than the physical challenges. It's natural to experience hunger or discomfort during a fast, but let those physical sensations remind you of your greater spiritual hunger for God.

In Matthew 4:4, Jesus said, "It is written, 'Man shall not live by bread alone, but by every word that proceeds from the mouth of God.'" As you fast, let this truth anchor your mindset. Focus on feasting on God's Word, His presence, and His promises, rather than on the absence of physical food.

4) **Persevere with Patience and Endurance**

Fasting can be challenging, especially if you are fasting for an extended period. It's important to approach your fast with a mindset of perseverance, knowing that spiritual growth often comes through enduring difficulty. Don't quit halfway. See it through.

Romans 5:3-4 reminds us, "And not only *that*, but we also glory in tribulations, knowing that tribulation produces perseverance; and perseverance, character; and character, hope." As you persevere through your fast, trust that God is developing your character, deepening your faith, and producing hope within you.

Eliminating Distractions and Focusing on God

One of the biggest challenges during a fast is maintaining focus on God amidst the distractions of daily life. To maximize the spiritual impact of your fast, it's important to identify and eliminate distractions that could hinder your time with God.

1) **Identify Potential Distractions**

Before you begin your fast, take some time to identify potential distractions that could pull your focus away from God. These might include:

- **Media and entertainment:** Television, social media, and other forms of entertainment can easily consume your time and attention, leaving little room for prayer and reflection.
- **Work and responsibilities:** While it's important to fulfill your daily responsibilities, be mindful of how work and other obligations might encroach on your time with God during the fast.
- **Social engagements:** Social activities, while enjoyable, can sometimes be a distraction during a fast, especially if they involve food or other temptations.

Once you've identified these potential distractions, make a plan to minimize or eliminate them during your fast.

2) **Create a Sacred Space for Your Fast**

Creating a sacred space for your fast can help you stay focused on God. This space doesn't have to be a physical location, although setting aside a quiet place for prayer and reflection can be helpful. It's more about creating an atmosphere in your heart and mind where you can connect with God without distractions.

Consider the following steps to create your sacred space:
- **Set boundaries:** Establish boundaries around your time with God during the fast. Let others know that you are fasting and may need some space for prayer and reflection.
- **Simplify your schedule:** If possible, simplify your schedule during the fast to allow for more time with God. This might mean saying no to certain activities or commitments.
- **Disconnect from media:** Consider taking a break from social media, television, and other forms of media during your fast. Use the time you would normally spend on these activities to focus on prayer, worship, and Scripture.

3) **Prioritize Time with God**

The most important aspect of your fast is your time with God. Prioritize this time above all else. Whether it's early in the morning, during lunch breaks, or in the evening, make sure you are carving out dedicated time each day to connect with God.

In Matthew 6:33, Jesus said, "But seek first the kingdom of God and His righteousness, and all these things shall be added to you." As you prioritize time with God during your fast, trust that He will meet you, guide you, and provide for all your needs.

PREPARING YOUR HEART AND MIND FOR A TRANSFORMATIVE FAST

Preparing for a fast is as important as the fast itself. By setting clear spiritual goals, creating a detailed fasting plan, cultivating the right mindset, and eliminating distractions, you can lay the foundation for a successful and transformative fasting experience.

Remember that fasting is not just about abstaining from food or other comforts—it's about drawing closer to God, seeking His presence, and allowing Him to work in your life in powerful ways. As you prepare for your fast, invite the Holy Spirit to guide you, strengthen you, and reveal to you what He wants to accomplish during this time.

May your fast be a time of deep spiritual growth, renewed intimacy with God, and transformative encounters with His presence, and may you emerge from your fast with a greater sense of His love, purpose, and calling for your life.

CHAPTER 8

OPTIMIZING YOUR FAST

DEEPENING YOUR SPIRITUAL EXPERIENCE

Optimizing your fast is about more than just abstaining from food; it's about creating a meaningful rhythm of prayer, reflection, and intentional growth. If you're looking to deepen your experience, the *Fasting Companion* book and app have been designed to walk you through a structured twenty-one-day fasting strategy. These resources provide daily prompts, prayer points, and journaling space to help you stay spiritually engaged and focused.

Fasting is more than just abstaining from food or other physical comforts; it is a time to deepen your relationship with God, hear His voice more clearly, and align your heart with His will. To fully experience the spiritual benefits of fasting, it's essential to be intentional about how you engage with God during this time. This chapter will provide strategies for optimizing your fast through prayer, journaling, scriptural meditation, and other spiritual practices. We will also explore how to receive insights and revelations during your fast and offer encouragement to help you stay committed and spiritually engaged throughout the journey.

MAXIMIZING SPIRITUAL BENEFITS: STRATEGIES FOR PRAYER, JOURNALING, AND SCRIPTURAL MEDITATION

The key to a fruitful fast lies in how you connect with God during this time. By intentionally engaging in prayer, journaling, and scriptural meditation, you can maximize the spiritual benefits of your fast and ensure that it becomes a transformative experience.

Establishing Prayer Points

Prayer is the cornerstone of any fast. To optimize your fast, it's essential to establish clear and focused prayer points that align with your spiritual goals. These prayer points will guide your time with God, ensuring that your prayers are intentional and directed.

Creating Effective Prayer Points:

- **Start with your spiritual goals:** Reflect on the spiritual goals you set at the beginning of your fast. What are the specific areas in your life where you need God's guidance, intervention, or breakthrough? Your prayer points should be directly tied to these goals.
- **Use Scripture as a foundation:** Scripture provides a powerful foundation for your prayers. Identify Bible verses that relate to your prayer points and incorporate them into your prayers. This practice grounds your requests in God's Word and aligns your desires with His promises.

Suggested Prayer Points:

Prayer for Spiritual Renewal:
- **Scripture Reference:** Psalm 51:10: "Create in me a clean heart, O God, and renew a steadfast spirit within me."

- **Prayer Point:** Ask God to renew your heart and spirit during the fast, cleansing you from anything that hinders your relationship with Him. Pray for a deeper intimacy with God and a fresh outpouring of the Holy Spirit in your life.

Prayer for Guidance and Direction:
- **Scripture Reference:** Proverbs 3:5-6: "Trust in the LORD with all your heart, And lean not on your own understanding; in all your ways acknowledge Him, and He shall direct your paths."
- **Prayer Point:** Seek God's wisdom and direction in your life. Ask Him to guide your decisions, to open doors that align with His will, and to close those that do not. Pray for clarity and confidence in following His lead.

Prayer for Breaking Strongholds:
- **Scripture Reference:** 2 Corinthians 10:4-5: "For the weapons of our warfare are not carnal but mighty in God for pulling down strongholds, casting down arguments and every high thing that exalts itself against the knowledge of God, bringing every thought into captivity to the obedience of Christ."
- **Prayer Point:** Pray for the breaking of any strongholds in your life—whether they are sinful habits, addictions, or negative thought patterns. Ask God to give you the strength to overcome these barriers and to live in the freedom that Christ offers.

Prayer for Intercession:
- **Scripture Reference:** 1 Timothy 2:1: "Therefore I exhort first of all that supplications, prayers, intercessions, and giving of thanks be made for all men."
- **Prayer Point:** Stand in the gap for others by interceding for your family, friends, church, and community. Pray for their spiritual growth and protection and for God's will to be done in their

lives. Ask God to use you as a vessel of His love and grace to those around you.

Prayer for Healing and Restoration:
- **Scripture Reference:** Jeremiah 30:17: "For I will restore health to you and heal you of your wounds,' says the LORD."
- **Prayer Point:** Pray for physical, emotional, and spiritual healing for yourself and others. Ask God to restore what has been broken or lost, and to bring complete healing and wholeness to every area of your life.

Journaling: Recording Your Spiritual Journey

Journaling is a powerful tool for documenting your spiritual journey during a fast. By writing down your prayers, insights, and what God is revealing to you, you create a record of your experience that you can refer to in the future.

Benefits of Journaling During a Fast:
- **Tracking progress:** Journaling allows you to track your spiritual progress throughout the fast. You can see how your prayers are evolving, how God is answering them, and how your relationship with Him is deepening.
- **Receiving and recording revelations:** Often, God will speak to you during a fast through His Word, through prayer, or through inner impressions. Journaling gives you a place to record these revelations, ensuring that you don't forget them.
- **Processing emotions and struggles:** Fasting can bring up a range of emotions and spiritual struggles. Journaling provides a safe space to process these feelings, to pour out your heart to God, and to seek His comfort and guidance.

How to Journal Effectively:
- **Set aside time each day:** Dedicate time each day during your fast to journal. This could be during your prayer time or at the end of the day as you reflect on what God has been showing you.
- **Write freely:** Don't worry about grammar, spelling, or structure. Let your thoughts flow freely as you write down your prayers, reflections, and any insights or revelations you receive.
- **Include Scripture:** Incorporate Bible verses that resonate with what you're experiencing. This not only grounds your journaling in God's Word but also helps you meditate on Scripture.
- **Review and reflect:** Periodically review your journal entries during the fast. This helps you see patterns, track answered prayers and gain deeper insights into what God is doing in your life.

Scriptural Meditation: Feasting on God's Word

During a fast, physical food is set aside, but spiritual nourishment from God's Word becomes even more important. Scriptural meditation is the practice of deeply reflecting on Bible passages, allowing them to penetrate your heart and transform your thinking.

Steps for Scriptural Meditation:
- **Choose a passage:** Select a passage of Scripture that aligns with your spiritual goals or prayer points. This could be a single verse, a psalm, or a longer passage.
- **Read slowly and reflectively:** Read the passage slowly, pausing to reflect on each word or phrase. Consider what God is saying through the text and how it applies to your life.
- **Pray the Scripture:** Turn the passage into a prayer, asking God to make His Word come alive in your heart. For example, if you are meditating on Psalm 23:1, you might pray, "Lord, thank You

for being my Shepherd. Help me to trust You fully as You guide and provide for me."
- **Memorize key verses:** Choose key verses from your meditation to memorize. This allows you to carry God's Word with you throughout the day, continually drawing on its strength and wisdom.

Benefits of Scriptural Meditation:
- **Deepening understanding:** As you meditate on Scripture, you gain a deeper understanding of God's character, His promises, and His will for your life.
- **Spiritual nourishment:** Just as physical food sustains the body, God's Word sustains your spirit. Scriptural meditation provides the spiritual nourishment you need to stay strong during the fast.
- **Transformation of mind:** Romans 12:2 says, "And do not be conformed to this world, but be transformed by the renewing of your mind." Scriptural meditation renews your mind, helping you think more like Christ and align your thoughts with His truth.

RECEIVING INSIGHTS AND REVELATIONS DURING YOUR FAST

Fasting opens your spiritual senses, making you more attuned to hearing God's voice and receiving His revelations. As you engage in the practices of prayer, journaling, and scriptural meditation, be open to the insights and revelations that God may impart to you.

1) **Be Still and Listen**

One of the most important aspects of receiving insights and revelations during a fast is simply being still and listening. In our busy lives, it can be difficult to hear God's voice but fasting creates space for stillness and attentiveness.

Psalm 46:10 reminds us, "Be still, and know that I *am* God." During your fast, make time to sit quietly in God's presence, with no agenda other than to listen. This might be during your prayer time, after reading Scripture, or as you journal. Trust that God will speak to you in the stillness, whether through a Scripture verse, an inner prompting, or a sense of His presence.

2) **Pay Attention to Dreams and Visions**

Fasting can heighten your spiritual sensitivity, sometimes leading to dreams or visions. These experiences can be God's way of communicating with you, offering guidance, encouragement, or revelation.

Acts 2:17 says, "And it shall come to pass in the last days, says God, that I will pour out of My Spirit on all flesh; your sons and your daughters shall prophesy, your young men shall see visions, your old men shall dream dreams." Be attentive to any dreams or visions you have during your fast, and ask God for discernment in understanding their meaning.

3) **Seek God's Confirmation**

As you receive insights and revelations during your fast, it's important to seek God's confirmation. Not every thought or impression may be from the Lord, so take time to test what you hear against Scripture and in prayer.

1 John 4:1 advises, "Beloved, do not believe every spirit, but test the spirits, whether they are of God." Ask God to confirm His word to you through Scripture, through the counsel of mature believers, or through circumstances. Trust that He will provide clarity and assurance as you seek His will.

STAYING COMMITTED AND SPIRITUALLY ENGAGED

Fasting can be challenging, especially as you progress through longer periods of fasting. It's important to stay committed and spiritually engaged throughout the entire fast, even when you face difficulties or distractions.

1) **Focus on Your Spiritual Goals**

When the fast becomes difficult, remind yourself of the spiritual goals you set at the beginning. Reflect on why you are fasting and what you hope to achieve. Keeping your goals in mind will help you stay motivated and focused on the spiritual benefits rather than the physical challenges.

2) **Rely on God's Strength**

Fasting is not about relying on your own strength but on God's. Philippians 4:13 says, "I can do all things through Christ who strengthens me." When you feel weak or discouraged, turn to God for strength and endurance. Ask Him to carry you through the fast and to empower you to stay faithful.

3) **Stay Connected with a Supportive Community**

If possible, fast with others or stay connected with a supportive community during your fast. Sharing your experiences, praying together, and encouraging one another can make a significant difference in staying committed and spiritually engaged. The fasting companion app is a great place to find community.

Hebrews 10:24-25 encourages us, "And let us consider one another in order to stir up love and good works, not forsaking the assembling of ourselves together." Whether you're fasting as part of a church or with a small group, lean on your community for support and accountability.

EMBRACING THE FULLNESS OF YOUR FAST

Optimizing your fast involves more than just abstaining from food or other comforts; it requires intentional engagement with God through prayer, journaling, scriptural meditation, and attentiveness to His voice. By incorporating these practices into your fast, you can maximize the spiritual benefits and ensure that your fast becomes a time of deep spiritual growth and transformation.

As you move forward in your fasting journey, remember that God is faithful to meet you in your seeking. He will speak to you, guide you, and reveal His heart to you in ways that you may not have experienced before. Stay committed, stay engaged, and embrace the fullness of what God has for you during this sacred time of fasting. May your fast be a time of rich spiritual encounter, where you draw closer to God, hear His voice more clearly, and experience the transformative power of His presence.

CHAPTER 9

ENDURING IN YOUR FAST

THE JOURNEY OF PERSEVERANCE

Fasting is a spiritual discipline that requires not only a strong commitment to begin but also the perseverance to see it through to the end. As you progress in your fast, you may encounter physical, mental, and spiritual challenges that test your resolve. Enduring in your fast is about maintaining your focus on God, caring for your body, and overcoming the common struggles that may arise. In this chapter, we will explore practical advice on maintaining physical health, strategies for overcoming common struggles, and encouragement to help you persevere during extended fasts.

Maintaining Physical Health: Hydration, Rest, and Focus

While fasting is primarily a spiritual practice, it has a significant impact on your physical body. To endure in your fast, it's important to take care of your body by staying hydrated, getting enough rest, and maintaining focus on your spiritual goals.

1) **Hydration:** Keeping Your Body Nourished

One of the most crucial aspects of physical health during a fast is staying hydrated. Since you are abstaining from food, your body may become more susceptible to dehydration, especially if you are engaging in a complete or extended fast.

Tips for Staying Hydrated:

- **Drink water regularly:** Aim to drink water throughout the day, even if you're not feeling particularly thirsty. Sipping water consistently helps to keep your body hydrated and can reduce feelings of hunger.
- **Add electrolytes:** If you're engaging in a longer fast, consider adding electrolytes to your water to replenish essential minerals that your body loses during the fast. This can help prevent dehydration and maintain your energy levels.
- **Avoid diuretics:** Be mindful of beverages that can dehydrate you, such as caffeinated drinks or sugary sodas. These can increase your risk of dehydration and may make fasting more difficult.
- **Listen to your body:** Pay attention to signs of dehydration, such as dizziness, dry mouth, or dark urine. If you experience any of these symptoms, increase your water intake and rest until you feel better.

Staying hydrated is not just about caring for your physical body; it's also a way of honoring the vessel that God has given you. As you drink water, reflect on Jesus's words in John 4:14: "But whoever drinks of the water that I shall give him will never thirst. But the water that I shall give him will become in him a fountain of water springing up into everlasting life."

2) **Rest:** Allowing Your Body to Recharge

Fasting can take a toll on your physical energy, especially if you are abstaining from food for an extended period. To endure in your fast, it's essential to prioritize rest, allowing your body the time it needs to recharge and recover.

Tips for Resting During a Fast:
- **Schedule rest periods:** Plan specific times during your day for rest, whether it's a short nap, quiet time with God, or simply sitting in silence. This gives your body a chance to conserve energy and helps you stay focused on your spiritual goals.
- **Get adequate sleep:** Ensure that you are getting enough sleep each night. A well-rested body is better equipped to handle the physical challenges of fasting, and adequate sleep can also enhance your mental clarity and spiritual focus.
- **Practice gentle movement:** While it's important to rest, light physical activity such as walking or stretching can help keep your body limber and improve circulation. Avoid strenuous exercise that might deplete your energy reserves.
- **Embrace spiritual rest:** In addition to physical rest, prioritize spiritual rest by spending time in God's presence, meditating on Scripture, and allowing His peace to fill your heart. Jesus invites us in Matthew 11:28: "Come to Me, all you who labor and are heavy laden, and I will give you rest."

Rest is an essential component of enduring in your fast. By taking the time to rest, you allow your body to recover, which in turn helps you maintain the stamina needed to continue seeking God through your fast.

3) **Focus:** Keeping Your Mind on Spiritual Goals

Maintaining focus during a fast can be challenging, especially as you deal with physical hunger, mental fatigue, or external distractions. To endure in your fast, it's important to keep your mind fixed on your spiritual goals and the purpose of your fast.

Tips for Maintaining Focus:
- **Set daily intentions:** At the beginning of each day, set specific intentions for your fast. Reflect on what you hope to achieve spiritually and how you want to connect with God. This helps to orient your mind toward your spiritual goals from the start.
- **Limit distractions:** Identify and minimize potential distractions that could pull your focus away from God. This might involve setting boundaries around your use of technology, reducing your exposure to media, or creating a quiet space for prayer and reflection.
- **Engage in spiritual practices:** Use your fasting time to engage in spiritual practices such as prayer, worship, journaling, and reading Scripture. These activities help to keep your mind focused on God and deepen your spiritual experience.
- **Remind yourself of the purpose:** Regularly remind yourself why you are fasting. Reflect on the spiritual goals you set at the beginning of your fast and the ways you are seeking God's presence, guidance, or intervention.

As you maintain your focus, remember the words of Philippians 4:8:
Finally, brethren, whatever things are true, whatever things are noble, whatever things are just, whatever things are pure, whatever things are lovely, whatever things are of good report, if there is any virtue and if there is anything praiseworthy—meditate on these things.

By keeping your mind on the things of God, you can endure in your fast with purpose and clarity.

Overcoming Common Struggles and Temptations While Fasting

Fasting often brings with it certain struggles and temptations that can challenge your commitment. Whether it's physical hunger, mental fatigue, or spiritual opposition, it's important to have strategies in place to overcome these challenges and stay faithful to your fast.

1) **Dealing with Physical Hunger**

Hunger is one of the most common challenges during a fast, especially in the early stages. It can be distracting and even discouraging, but it's important to remember that hunger is a natural part of the fasting process.

Strategies for Managing Hunger:

- **Stay hydrated:** As mentioned earlier, drinking water can help alleviate feelings of hunger. Sometimes, thirst can be mistaken for hunger, so staying hydrated is key.
- **Focus on spiritual hunger:** Use physical hunger as a reminder of your spiritual hunger for God. Every time you feel hungry, take it as an opportunity to turn your thoughts toward God and to seek His presence more deeply.
- **Distract yourself with spiritual activities:** When hunger pangs hit, engage in spiritual activities such as prayer, worship, or reading Scripture. This helps to shift your focus from your physical hunger to your spiritual goals.
- **Embrace the discomfort:** Fasting is meant to be a time of self-denial and reliance on God. Embrace the discomfort of hunger as part of the fasting experience and trust that God will sustain you.

Remember Jesus's words in Matthew 4:4: "It is written, 'Man shall not live by bread alone, but by every word that proceeds from the mouth of God.'" Let this truth guide you as you navigate the challenges of physical hunger during your fast.

2) **Overcoming Mental Fatigue and Discouragement**

Mental fatigue and discouragement can set in, especially during longer fasts. You may find your thoughts wandering, or you may start to question the value of your fast. It's important to recognize these challenges and address them with intentionality.

Strategies for Battling Mental Fatigue:

- **Renew your mind with Scripture:** Use God's Word to refresh your mind. Memorize and meditate on verses that encourage perseverance and endurance, such as Isaiah 40:31: "But those who wait on the LORD shall renew their strength; they shall mount up with wings like eagles, they shall run and not be weary, they shall walk and not faint."

- **Take breaks when needed:** If you find yourself mentally fatigued, it's okay to take short breaks to rest your mind. Step away from your regular activities, close your eyes, and breathe deeply. This can help clear your mind and refocus your thoughts on God.

- **Seek encouragement from others:** If you're fasting with others, share your struggles and ask for their prayers and encouragement. Sometimes, just knowing that others are praying for you can lift your spirits and help you stay committed.

Mental fatigue and discouragement are natural parts of the fasting journey, but by renewing your mind with Scripture and seeking support, you can overcome these challenges and stay focused on your spiritual goals.

3) **Resisting Temptations to Break the Fast**
As you progress in your fast, you may encounter temptations to break it early, especially if the fast becomes physically or emotionally challenging. It's important to resist these temptations and to stay committed to the duration and purpose of your fast.

Strategies for Resisting Temptation:
- **Remind yourself of the commitment:** Reflect on the commitment you made at the beginning of your fast. Remind yourself of the reasons you are fasting and the spiritual goals you hope to achieve. This can help you resist the urge to give up prematurely.
- **Pray for strength:** Whenever you feel tempted to break your fast, turn to God in prayer. Ask Him for the strength and resolve to continue, and trust that He will sustain you.
- **Consider the consequences:** Think about the potential spiritual and emotional consequences of breaking your fast early. Consider how it might impact your relationship with God and your sense of spiritual accomplishment. This reflection can help you stay on track.

James 1:12 offers a promise for those who endure temptation: "Blessed *is* the man who endures temptation; for when he has been approved, he will receive the crown of life which the Lord has promised to those who love Him." Keep this promise in mind as you resist the temptations to break your fast.

ENCOURAGEMENT FOR PERSEVERANCE DURING EXTENDED FASTS

Extended fasts, such as those lasting twenty-one or forty days, require a higher level of perseverance and endurance. As the days go by, you may find the challenges intensifying, but it's during these times that spiritual breakthroughs often occur. Here's how to stay strong and persevere during an extended fast.

1) **Lean on God's Strength, Not Your Own**

During an extended fast, it's crucial to remember that your strength comes from God, not from your own efforts. As you progress in your fast, continually rely on God's power to sustain you.

Philippians 4:13 reminds us, "I can do all things through Christ who strengthens me." When you feel weary or tempted to give up, declare this verse over yourself and trust that God will provide the strength you need to persevere.

2) **Reflect on Past Victories**

One way to stay encouraged during an extended fast is to reflect on past victories—times when God has brought you through difficult situations or answered your prayers. Reminding yourself of God's faithfulness in the past can give you the confidence to continue pressing forward.

Consider keeping a "victory journal" where you record instances of God's faithfulness in your life. During your fast, revisit these entries and let them remind you of God's goodness and power.

3) **Focus on the Finish Line**

As you approach the final days of your fast, focus on the finish line and the spiritual breakthrough that awaits you. Visualize the joy of completing your fast and the sense of accomplishment you will feel. More importantly, anticipate the deeper relationship with God and the answers to prayer that may come as a result.

2 Timothy 4:7 captures the spirit of perseverance: "I have fought the good fight, I have finished the race, I have kept the faith." Let this verse inspire you to finish your fast strong, knowing that you are running a race that will lead to spiritual rewards.

EMBRACING THE STRENGTH TO ENDURE

Enduring in your fast is about more than just surviving the physical challenges; it's about embracing the strength that comes from God to persevere through difficulties and to experience the spiritual growth that fasting brings. By maintaining your physical health through hydration, rest, and focus, overcoming common struggles, and leaning on God's strength, you can successfully complete your fast and reap the spiritual benefits.

As you journey through your fast, remember that you are not alone. God is with you every step of the way, providing the strength, encouragement, and grace you need to endure. Stay committed, stay focused, and trust that God will bring you through to the end with greater spiritual insight, deeper intimacy with Him, and a renewed sense of purpose.

Let your fast be a time of spiritual endurance, where you experience the power of God's sustaining grace and emerge stronger in your faith.

CHAPTER 10

BREAKING YOUR FAST

A THOUGHTFUL CONCLUSION TO A SACRED JOURNEY

As you approach the end of your fast, you are standing at a significant moment of transition. The journey you've been on—seeking God, refining your focus, and aligning your heart with His will—has been one of spiritual depth and personal transformation. Breaking your fast is not merely about resuming eating; it is a sacred moment that calls for mindfulness and care.

This chapter explores how to break your fast in a way that honors both your body and spirit. Reintroducing food after an extended fast requires a thoughtful approach, grounded not only in spiritual wisdom but also in scientific understanding. The decisions you make during this transition can have lasting effects on your physical health and spiritual well-being.

For those seeking more detailed guidance, the *Fasting Companion* and the app provide an in-depth discussion on breaking your fast, offering step-by-step strategies and practical advice based on both spiritual principles and scientific insights.

Reintroducing Food Safely: A Gentle Approach

After a period of fasting, your body has adapted to going without food, and your digestive system has had the chance to rest and reset. This pause in digestion is beneficial, but it also means that your body requires a gradual reintroduction to food. Scientific research underscores the importance of easing back into eating to avoid overwhelming your system, which could lead to discomfort or even more serious complications.

Start Slow and Simple. When you begin eating again, it's crucial to start with small portions of easily digestible foods. Light, nourishing options like broths, smoothies, or steamed vegetables are ideal. These choices are not only gentle on your digestive system but also rich in nutrients that your body can readily absorb.

In his book, *The Complete Guide to Fasting*, Dr. Jason Fung, a leading expert in intermittent fasting, emphasizes the importance of reintroducing food gradually. He suggests starting with simple liquids and progressing slowly to solid foods, giving your digestive system time to adjust.[1] Similarly, research published in Pediatric Clinics, 2009 advises that refeeding after an extended fast should be approached with caution to prevent refeeding syndrome, a potentially dangerous shift in fluids and electrolytes.

Here's a recommended strategy for safely reintroducing food after an extended fast:

1) **Days One and Two:** Begin with clear broths, diluted fruit juices, and light smoothies. These liquids provide hydration and essential nutrients while being gentle on your stomach. Avoid solid

---

[1] Jason Fung, *The Complete Guide to Fasting: Heal Your Body Through Intermittent, Alternate-Day, and Extended Fasting* (Las Vegas, NV: Victory Belt Publishing, 2016).

foods during this initial phase to allow your digestive system to ease back into processing nourishment.

2) **Days Three and Four:** Gradually introduce soft, easily digestible foods like steamed vegetables, mashed potatoes, or soft fruits such as bananas. You might also incorporate small amounts of plain yogurt or soft-cooked grains like oatmeal, which are easy to digest and gentle on your system.

3) **Days Five through Seven:** As your body adjusts, you can begin to reintroduce lean proteins such as fish or chicken, along with more solid vegetables and whole grains. Continue to avoid heavy, fatty, or highly processed foods, as these can be difficult for your body to handle immediately after a fast.

4) **Beyond Day Seven:** Gradually return to your regular diet while continuing to prioritize balanced, nutritious meals. Consider maintaining some of the healthier eating habits you developed during your fast, such as increased intake of fruits and vegetables, to support ongoing physical and spiritual well-being.

This reintroduction strategy is designed to help your body transition smoothly back to eating, minimizing the risk of digestive discomfort or other complications.

Listen to Your Body. Your body will communicate with you during this transition. You might notice that you feel full more quickly than usual, or that certain foods don't sit well initially. Pay attention to these signals and adjust your eating habits accordingly. If you experience any discomfort, slow down and give your body more time to adjust.

Hydration Remains Essential. Hydration continues to be crucial as you reintroduce food. Drinking plenty of water throughout the day aids in digestion and helps your body adapt to processing food again. Herbal teas or diluted fruit juices can also provide gentle hydration and essential nutrients, supporting your body's transition back to regular eating.

THE SPIRITUAL AND PHYSICAL IMPORTANCE OF ENDING WELL

Breaking your fast is both a physical and spiritual act. This moment of transition is an opportunity to reflect on the journey you've just completed, to honor the spiritual growth you've experienced, and to ensure that the benefits of your fast continue into your daily life.

Reflect on Your Journey. Before you take that first bite, pause for a moment of prayer and gratitude. Thank God for sustaining you throughout your fast, for the insights and revelations He has given you, and for the strength He provided during challenging moments. This act of thanksgiving not only honors God but also helps you internalize the spiritual lessons of your fast.

Consider Journaling about Your Experience. Document the challenges you faced, the breakthroughs you experienced, and the ways in which your relationship with God has deepened. This reflection can serve as a lasting reminder of God's faithfulness and can inspire you to maintain the spiritual disciplines you developed during your fast.

Transitioning Back with Intention. As you return to your regular routine, think about how you can maintain the spiritual habits you cultivated during your fast. Perhaps you spent more time in prayer, engaged in deeper Scripture study, or made room for quiet reflection. Consider how you can continue these practices in your daily life, allowing the spiritual growth you experienced during your fast to continue to flourish.

The end of your fast is not just about resuming your normal diet; it's about carrying forward the spiritual clarity and discipline you gained.

As you transition back, keep in mind the words of 1 Corinthians 10:31: "Therefore, whether you eat or drink, or whatever you do, do all to the glory of God." Let this mindset guide your choices, not just in what you eat, but in how you live.

GUIDELINES FOR MAINTAINING THE BENEFITS OF YOUR FAST

Fasting often brings about positive changes in your life, both spiritually and physically. The challenge now is to sustain those benefits and allow them to continue shaping your life in meaningful ways by doing the following:

1) **Establish New Habits**

During your fast, you may have developed new routines or disciplines that drew you closer to God. Whether it was increased prayer time, regular Scripture reading, or moments of stillness, these habits don't have to end when the fast does. Think about how you can continue these practices and integrate them into your everyday life.

For example, if you developed a habit of journaling your prayers and thoughts, consider continuing this practice as a way to keep track of your spiritual journey and stay connected to God's ongoing work in your life.

2) **Guard the Ground You've Gained**

Fasting often brings clarity, freedom from distractions, and a renewed focus on God. It's important to guard this newfound clarity and not let old habits or distractions creep back in. Set boundaries that protect your spiritual priorities—whether it's limiting time spent on social media, setting aside daily quiet time with God, or being mindful of what you consume, both physically and spiritually.

3) Stay Connected to Community

Fasting often brings us closer to God, but it can also strengthen our connections with others. Whether you fasted with a group or received support from friends and family, these relationships are valuable for your continued spiritual growth. Share your experiences, insights, and struggles with others, and seek ways to support one another in maintaining the benefits of your fast.

CONCLUSION: A NEW BEGINNING

Breaking your fast is more than just the end of a period of abstention; it's the beginning of a new chapter in your spiritual journey. How you approach this moment can set the tone for the days, weeks, and months ahead. By reintroducing food with care, reflecting on your spiritual journey, and maintaining the habits and insights you've gained, you can ensure that the benefits of your fast extend far beyond the fasting period.

As you transition back to your regular routine, remain open to the ongoing work that God wants to do in your life. The fast may be over, but the spiritual growth, clarity, and connection you've gained can continue to flourish. May this moment of breaking your fast be filled with gratitude, reflection, and anticipation for all that God has in store for you as you move forward in your journey of faith.

CHAPTER 11

SUSTAINING THE SPIRITUAL AND PHYSICAL GAINS OF FASTING

THE JOURNEY BEYOND THE FAST

Congratulations on taking a successfully concluded fast. Fasting is a powerful tool for spiritual growth and physical renewal, but the true value of a fast lies in what happens after it. The gains you've made during your fast, both spiritual and physical, are not meant to be fleeting. They are meant to be sustained and built upon as you continue your journey with God. In this chapter, we will explore how to live a fasted life, maintain spiritual discipline, and preserve the physical benefits of fasting. We'll also discuss the importance of consecration, ongoing spiritual vigilance, and the power of staying connected to a like-minded community.

Living a Fasted Life: A Continuous Walk in Discipline

The concept of living a fasted life extends beyond the days when you're actively fasting. It's about incorporating the principles of fasting self-discipline, intentionality, and a focus on God into your everyday life. This way of living is not about constant deprivation but about maintaining a posture of humility and dependence on God, allowing the spiritual gains from your fast to permeate every aspect of your life.

Maintaining Spiritual Discipline. During your fast, you likely developed new habits that deepened your relationship with God. Perhaps you spent more time in prayer, engaged in deeper study of Scripture, or practiced greater mindfulness in your daily actions. The key to sustaining these gains is to continue these practices even after the fast ends. Consider setting aside specific times each day for prayer and meditation. These moments of connection with God can serve as a foundation for your day, helping you maintain the spiritual clarity and focus you achieved during your fast. The Bible encourages us to "pray without ceasing" (1 Thessalonians 5:17), which can be understood as maintaining a continual awareness of God's presence and being in constant communion with Him.

Applying the Discipline of Fasting to Other Areas. The discipline you've built during your fast can also be applied to other areas of your life. For example, you might choose to fast from certain activities or distractions that hinder your spiritual growth, such as excessive social media use or unproductive habits. By setting these boundaries, you create more space for God to work in your life. Living a fasted life is about making choices that honor God and reflect the priorities you established during your fast. It's about consistently choosing what is beneficial for your spiritual and physical well-being, even when it requires sacrifice or discipline.

Consecration: Setting Yourself Apart for Ongoing Spiritual Growth

Consecration is the act of setting yourself apart for God's purposes. It involves dedicating yourself to a life of holiness, where your thoughts, actions, and desires are aligned with God's will. After a fast, consecration is a powerful way to sustain the spiritual growth you've experienced and to continue deepening your relationship with God.

The Role of Consecration in Spiritual Growth. Consecration involves a deliberate commitment to live in a way that honors God. It means being mindful of the choices you make and ensuring that they reflect your commitment to holiness. This might involve setting aside regular times for worship and study, being intentional about the media you consume, or dedicating yourself to serving others in love. In Romans 12:1, Paul urges believers to "present your bodies a living sacrifice, holy, acceptable to God, *which is* your reasonable service." This verse encapsulates the essence of consecration—offering yourself fully to God, not just in moments of fasting but in your daily life.

Practical Steps for Consecration:

- **Daily devotion:** Dedicate time each day to reading Scripture and praying, allowing God's Word to shape your thoughts and actions.
- **Mindful living:** Be intentional about the choices you make, from the words you speak to the way you spend your time. Ask yourself if these choices reflect your commitment to living a consecrated life.
- **Service to others:** Consecration is not just about personal holiness but also about loving and serving others. Look for opportunities to demonstrate God's love through acts of kindness, service, and compassion.

By setting yourself apart in these ways, you create an environment where ongoing spiritual growth is nurtured and sustained.

The gains you've made during your fast, whether spiritual, physical, or both, require ongoing vigilance to maintain. Spiritual vigilance involves being aware of the enemy's attempts to distract or derail you from your spiritual path. It also involves being proactive in maintaining the spiritual habits you developed during your fast.

Maintaining Spiritual Vigilance. Fasting often brings clarity and focus, but these gains can be quickly lost if you're not vigilant. The Bible warns us to "be sober, be vigilant; because your adversary the devil walks about like a roaring lion, seeking whom he may devour" (1 Peter 5:8). This verse reminds us that spiritual vigilance is necessary to guard the progress we've made.

Here are some ways to maintain spiritual vigilance:

- **Stay Rooted in Scripture:** Regularly reading and meditating on God's Word keeps your mind and heart aligned with His truth. It helps you recognize when you're being led astray by falsehoods or distractions.
- **Pray for discernment:** Ask God for the discernment to recognize and resist temptations that could undermine the spiritual gains you've made. Stay connected to Him through prayer, seeking His guidance in all areas of your life.
- **Surround yourself with encouragement:** Stay connected to a community of believers who can encourage and support you in your spiritual journey. Share your struggles and victories with them and be open to receiving their prayers and counsel.

Caring for Your Physical Health. Fasting often brings physical benefits, such as improved digestion, detoxification, and increased energy levels. To maintain these benefits, it's important to continue caring for your body after the fast. Consider incorporating healthy eating habits into your daily routine, prioritizing whole, nutritious foods that support your physical well-being. Regular exercise and sufficient rest are also crucial for maintaining the physical vitality you gained during your fast.

Remember that your body is a temple of the Holy Spirit (1 Corinthians 6:19), and caring for it is an act of worship. By maintaining your physical health, you honor God and create a strong foundation for ongoing spiritual growth.

The Power of Connectedness to a Like-Minded Community

One of the most powerful ways to sustain the gains from your fast is to stay connected to a community of like-minded believers. Fasting is often a solitary journey, but the spiritual growth you've experienced can be multiplied when you share it with others.

The Role of Community in Spiritual Growth. A community of believers provides encouragement, accountability, and support. They can help you stay focused on your spiritual goals and offer prayers and counsel when you face challenges. The Bible encourages us to "exhort one another daily" (Hebrews 3:13), reminding us of the importance of mutual encouragement in our spiritual journeys.

Being part of a community also allows you to share the insights and revelations you received during your fast. Your experiences can inspire and encourage others, and their experiences can, in turn, enrich your spiritual life.

Building and Maintaining Community Connections:

- **Join a small group:** If you're not already part of a small group or Bible study, consider joining one. These groups provide a space for deeper discussion, prayer, and mutual support.
- **Engage in corporate worship:** Regularly attending church services and participating in corporate worship keeps you connected to the larger body of Christ and strengthens your sense of belonging.
- **Serve together:** Look for opportunities to serve alongside other believers. Whether it's through volunteer work, ministry involvement, or community outreach, serving together deepens your connections and reinforces your commitment to living out your faith.

A LIFELONG COMMITMENT TO GROWTH

The end of your fast is not the end of your spiritual journey; it's a new beginning. Sustaining the spiritual and physical gains of fasting requires ongoing commitment, discipline, and vigilance. By living a fasted life, dedicating yourself to ongoing consecration, maintaining spiritual and physical health, and staying connected to a like-minded community, you can ensure that the benefits of your fast continue to bear fruit in your life. As you move forward, remember that spiritual growth is a lifelong journey. Each day presents new opportunities to draw closer to God, to deepen your faith, and to live out the principles you embraced during your fast. *The Fasting Companion Workbook* offers additional resources and strategies to help you sustain these gains, with practical advice and exercises designed to support your continued spiritual growth.

May the lessons you've learned during your fast continue to shape your life, guiding you into deeper intimacy with God and greater effectiveness in your walk with Him. As you live out these principles, may you experience the fullness of God's blessings and the ongoing transformation that comes from a life dedicated to His purposes.

PART 2

The Science of Fasting

As we transition to Part 2 of this journey, it's important to recognize that fasting is a practice that deeply intertwines both the spiritual and the physical. While the first part of this book has focused on the spiritual discipline of fasting and its power to draw us closer to God, refine our spirits, and align us with His will, the second part will delve into the science behind fasting, exploring how this ancient practice also benefits our physical bodies.

Fasting is a holistic discipline. Just as it cultivates spiritual clarity and renewal, it also has profound effects on our physical health. In fact, the physical benefits of fasting can enhance our spiritual practice, creating a harmonious balance between body and spirit. When we fast, we're not just denying ourselves food; we're engaging in a process that touches every part of our being, spirit, mind, and body. Understanding the science of fasting doesn't diminish its spiritual significance. Rather, it enriches our appreciation of the practice, revealing the wisdom of God's design for our bodies. By exploring the physiological processes that occur during fasting, such as detoxification, cell regeneration, and improved metabolic health, we gain insight into how fasting can be a powerful tool for overall well-being.

This next section is not a departure from the spiritual focus of fasting, but rather an extension of it. It's an opportunity to see how the physical and spiritual benefits of fasting are interconnected, each reinforcing the other. As we dive into the scientific aspects of fasting, let us remember that our bodies are temples of the Holy Spirit (1 Corinthians 6:19), and caring for them is an act of worship. By understanding how fasting impacts our physical health, we can approach this practice with even greater reverence and intentionality.

So, let's continue this journey, exploring the incredible design of our bodies and the remarkable ways fasting supports both our spiritual growth and physical vitality. May this deeper understanding of fasting inspire you to embrace it as a comprehensive practice that honors God with your whole being, spirit, soul, and body.

CHAPTER 12

UNDERSTANDING THE SCIENCE OF FASTING

OVERVIEW OF SCIENTIFIC RESEARCH ON FASTING

Fasting is not a new concept; it has been practiced for millennia across various cultures and religions. However, it is only in recent decades that science has begun to catch up with ancient wisdom, providing empirical evidence for the benefits of fasting. Researchers have conducted numerous studies to understand the effects of fasting on the body, and the results have been nothing short of remarkable.

The scientific community has identified several key areas where fasting has a profound impact: metabolic health, cellular repair, brain function, and longevity. These studies have been published in leading medical and scientific journals, and they offer a wealth of knowledge that can help us better understand how fasting works on a physiological level. There are four key areas where the most impact happens when fasting protocols are engaged.

1) **Metabolic Health:** Fasting has been shown to improve metabolic health by lowering blood sugar levels, reducing insulin

resistance, and promoting fat loss. These benefits are crucial for preventing and managing conditions such as type 2 diabetes, obesity, and cardiovascular disease.[1]

2) **Cellular Repair and Detoxification:** One of the most significant discoveries in fasting research is the process of autophagy, a cellular "clean up" process that is activated during fasting. Autophagy helps remove damaged cells and proteins from the body, promoting cellular repair, regeneration and longevity. This process is critical for preventing the accumulation of cellular waste that can lead to various diseases, including cancer and neurodegenerative disorders.[2]

3) **Brain Function and Mental Clarity:** Fasting has also been linked to improved brain function and mental clarity. Studies have shown that fasting can enhance cognitive function, protect against neurodegenerative diseases, and improve mood and mental well-being. These benefits are attributed to the production of brain-derived neurotrophic factor (BDNF) and the reduction of oxidative stress in the brain.[3]

4) **Longevity:** Perhaps one of the most exciting areas of research is the potential for fasting to extend lifespan. Animal studies have demonstrated that fasting can increase longevity by reducing the incidence of age-related diseases and promoting cellular repair. While more research is needed in humans, the findings suggest that fasting could be a powerful tool for promoting healthy aging.[4]

In the following sections, we will explore these areas in greater detail, examining the specific mechanisms through which fasting exerts its benefits and how these findings align with the spiritual practice of fasting.

THE PHYSICAL BENEFITS OF FASTING: DETOXIFICATION, CELLULAR REPAIR, AND LONGEVITY

Fasting is often viewed as a spiritual discipline, a time to draw closer to God and seek His guidance. However, it is also a powerful tool for physical health. When we fast, our bodies undergo a series of physiological changes that promote detoxification, cellular repair, and longevity. Understanding these processes can deepen our appreciation for fasting and encourage us to incorporate it more regularly into our lives.

Detoxification: The Body's Natural Cleansing Process

Detoxification is the process by which the body eliminates toxins and waste products. Our bodies are equipped with organs like the liver and kidneys that perform detoxification continuously. Fasting therefore enhances this process by giving these organs a break from processing food and allowing them to focus on clearing out accumulated toxins. During a fast, the body shifts its energy from digesting food to repairing and detoxifying cells, which is especially important in our modern world filled with environmental toxins and processed foods.

Scientific studies on mice subjects have shown that fasting can increase the efficiency of the liver's detoxification processes. Research published in *Cell Reports* found that fasting can enhance the activity of liver enzymes responsible for detoxifying harmful substances as well as reducing oxidative stress, which is a key factor in the development of chronic diseases.

Cellular Repair: Autophagy and Regeneration

One of the most remarkable discoveries in fasting research is the process of autophagy. Autophagy, derived from the Greek words for "self" and "eating," is the body's way of cleaning out damaged cells and regenerating new ones. This process is crucial for maintaining cellular health and preventing the accumulation of cellular waste that can lead to diseases. Autophagy is a natural process that occurs at a low level in the body, but it is significantly enhanced during fasting.

Dr. Yoshinori Ohsumi, a Japanese cell biologist, was awarded the Nobel Prize in Physiology or Medicine in 2016 for his groundbreaking research on autophagy. His studies revealed that fasting as a starvation protocol is one of the most effective ways to induce autophagy, which has profound implications for health and longevity. Autophagy has been linked to a range of health benefits, including the prevention of cancer, neurodegenerative diseases, and infections

By understanding the role of autophagy in fasting, individuals can incorporate longer or more frequent fasts to promote cellular repair and regeneration, aligning with both health and spiritual renewal principles.

There are also practical implications of autophagy. Understanding the role of autophagy in fasting can inspire us to embrace longer or more frequent fasts as a way to promote cellular repair and regeneration. While intermittent fasting can trigger autophagy, extended fasts (twenty-four to forty-eight hours or longer) may offer more significant benefits. Incorporating fasting into your routine with the intention of promoting autophagy can be a powerful tool for maintaining health and preventing disease. This practice aligns with the spiritual principle of renewal, as we allow our bodies to cleanse and regenerate just as we seek spiritual renewal through fasting.

Longevity: Extending Life Through Fasting
One of the most exciting areas of research on fasting is its potential to extend lifespan. Studies on animals have shown that fasting can increase longevity by promoting cellular repair, reducing the incidence of age-related diseases and improving metabolic health. These findings have sparked interest in fasting as a strategy for healthy aging.

Research on caloric restriction, a form of fasting where calorie intake is reduced without malnutrition, has consistently shown that it can extend lifespan in various species, including yeast, worms, and mice. The mechanisms behind this effect are believed to be similar to those triggered by fasting, including autophagy, reduced oxidative stress, and improved metabolic function.[5]

Dr. Valter Longo, a leading researcher in the field of aging, has developed a fasting-mimicking diet that replicates the benefits of fasting while allowing some calorie intake. His research suggests that this approach can extend lifespan, reduce the risk of chronic diseases, and improve overall health.[6]

HOW FASTING POSITIVELY IMPACTS BRAIN FUNCTION AND MENTAL CLARITY

In addition to its benefits for physical health, fasting has been shown to have a profound impact on brain function and mental clarity. The brain is one of the most metabolically active organs in the body, and it responds to fasting in ways that enhance cognitive function, protect against neurodegenerative diseases, and improve mood

When we fast, our bodies enter a state of ketosis, where fat is converted into ketones, which serve as an alternative energy source for the brain. Ketones are a more efficient fuel for the brain than glucose, leading to enhanced cognitive function, improved focus, and increased mental clarity. Fasting has been shown to increase the production of brain-derived neurotrophic factor (BDNF), a protein that plays a critical role in the growth and survival of neurons. BDNF supports cognitive function by promoting neurogenesis (the growth of new neurons) and synaptic plasticity (the ability of the brain to form and reorganize synaptic connections)

Research published in *Nature Reviews Neuroscience* has demonstrated that increased levels of BDNF are associated with improved memory, learning, and overall cognitive function.[7] BDNF also has a protective effect on the brain, reducing the risk of neurodegenerative diseases such as Alzheimer's and Parkinson's disease (Mattson, 2015).

Fasting also helps reduce oxidative stress in the brain, which is a key factor in the development of neurodegenerative diseases. Oxidative stress occurs when there is an imbalance between free radicals (unstable molecules that can damage cells) and antioxidants in the body. This imbalance can lead to inflammation and cell damage, particularly in the brain.[8]

Mental Clarity and Emotional Well-Being: The Psychological Benefits of Fasting

In addition to its cognitive benefits, fasting has been shown to improve mental clarity and emotional well-being. Many people who fast report a heightened sense of focus, clarity, and calm, which can be attributed to the effects of fasting on brain chemistry and neurotransmitter levels.[9]

The Impact of Fasting on Neurotransmitters: Fasting has been shown to influence the production of neurotransmitters, which are chemicals that transmit signals between nerve cells in the brain. Two key neurotransmitters affected by fasting are serotonin and dopamine, both of which play a significant role in mood regulation. Serotonin is often referred to as the "feel-good" neurotransmitter because it contributes to feelings of well-being and happiness. Fasting has been shown to increase serotonin levels, which can improve mood and reduce symptoms of depression and anxiety.[10] Dopamine, another important neurotransmitter, is associated with motivation, reward, and pleasure. Fasting can increase dopamine sensitivity, leading to enhanced motivation and focus.[11]

The Gut-Brain Axis: Fasting and Mental Health: Emerging research also points to the benefits of fasting for mental health, particularly through its effects on the gut-brain axis. The gut-brain axis is the communication network between your gut and your brain, and it plays a significant role in regulating mood and cognitive function. Fasting can positively influence the gut microbiome, the community of bacteria living in your digestive system. A healthy gut microbiome has been linked to improved mental health, reduced anxiety and depression, and enhanced cognitive function. A study published in *Nature Reviews Neuroscience* showed that fasting can modulate the gut microbiome, leading to these mental health benefits.[12]

Practical Implications for Mental Health: The mental health benefits of fasting are particularly relevant in today's fast-paced world, where stress, anxiety, and depression are increasingly common. By incorporating fasting into your routine, you can support your mental health and enhance your emotional well-being.

To maximize the mental health benefits of fasting, consider combining fasting with other practices that promote mental clarity and emotional well-being, such as meditation, mindfulness, and prayer. These practices can help you stay centered and focused during your fast, allowing you to fully experience the mental and emotional benefits of fasting.[13]

INTEGRATING SCIENCE AND SPIRITUALITY: A HOLISTIC APPROACH TO FASTING

Understanding the science of fasting enhances our appreciation of this ancient practice. The physical benefits of fasting are not separate from its spiritual significance; rather, they complement and reinforce each other. When we fast, we engage in a holistic discipline that nourishes both body and spirit. By embracing both the faith and the science of fasting, we can approach this practice with greater intentionality and understanding. The physiological processes that occur during fasting, such as detoxification, cellular repair, and enhanced brain function, are part of the intricate design that God has woven into our very being. These benefits support our spiritual practice, creating a deeper and more integrated experience of fasting.[14]

As we continue to explore the science behind fasting, let us remember that our bodies are temples of the Holy Spirit (1 Corinthians 6:19), and caring for them is an act of worship. By understanding how fasting impacts our physical health, we can approach this practice with even greater reverence and intentionality.[15]

THE SYNERGY OF SCIENCE AND FAITH IN FASTING

Fasting is a powerful practice that bridges the gap between the spiritual and the physical. As we have explored in this chapter, the scientific evidence supporting the benefits of fasting is extensive and compelling. From detoxification and cellular repair to enhanced brain function and longevity, fasting offers a wide range of health benefits that align with its spiritual significance.[16]

By understanding the science of fasting, we can deepen our appreciation for this ancient discipline and embrace it as a holistic practice that nourishes both our bodies and our spirits. The integration of science and faith in fasting allows us to approach this practice with confidence, knowing that we are honoring God with our whole being, spirit, mind, and body.

As we move forward in this journey, let us continue to explore the depths of fasting, drawing on both spiritual wisdom and scientific knowledge to guide us. For those interested in delving deeper into the research, a compilation of scientific journals and authors referenced throughout this section is provided at the end of the book.

May this knowledge empower you to embrace fasting as a transformative practice that brings you closer to God and supports your overall health and well-being.

CHAPTER 13

NEUROTHEOLOGY: THE INTERSECTION OF MIND, BODY, AND SPIRIT

THE EMERGING FIELD OF NEUROTHEOLOGY

In recent years, neurotheology has emerged as a fascinating field that sits at the crossroads of neuroscience and theology. This interdisciplinary study seeks to understand how spiritual practices such as prayer, meditation, and fasting affect the brain, providing a deeper understanding of the physiological underpinnings of our spiritual experiences. Neurotheology offers valuable insights into how these practices are not only rooted in our faith but also embedded in the intricate workings of our brain.[17]

One of the pioneering voices in this field is Dr. Andrew Newberg, whose research explores how religious and spiritual practices shape our brains. His work, particularly in *How God Changes Your Brain*, has significantly contributed to our understanding of the neurological effects of spirituality. For believers, neurotheology serves as a bridge between faith and science, affirming that our spiritual experiences are both profoundly meaningful and neurologically transformative.[18]

In this chapter, we will delve into the implications of neurotheology for fasting, examining how this practice, especially when combined with prayer, influences brain health, enhances spiritual experiences, and contributes to a holistic understanding of mind, body, and spirit.

The Growing Field of Neurotheology and Its Implications for Fasting

Neurotheology, sometimes referred to as the neuroscience of religion, is a multidisciplinary field that explores the relationship between brain function and spiritual experiences. Researchers like Andrew Newberg have used advanced imaging technologies, such as functional magnetic resonance imaging (fMRI) and positron emission tomography (PET), to study how religious practices affect brain activity. These studies have revealed that spiritual practices can significantly alter brain structure and function, enhancing mental health and deepening spiritual experiences.[19]

At its core, neurotheology posits that spiritual experiences are not only psychological but also deeply embedded in the brain's neural networks. Dr. Andrew Newberg's research has shown that practices like prayer and meditation can lead to measurable changes in the brain, particularly in areas related to attention, emotion, and self-perception.[20]

In *How God Changes Your Brain*, Newberg explains that spiritual practices can enhance the brain's neuroplasticity—the ability of the brain to reorganize itself by forming new neural connections. This adaptability allows the brain to grow and change in response to spiritual experiences, suggesting that our spiritual lives are intricately connected to our neurological health. The implications of neurotheology for fasting are profound. Fasting is not only a spiritual discipline but also a practice with measurable effects on brain health. Research suggests that fasting, particularly when combined with prayer, can influence the brain's neural pathways, enhancing cognitive function and deepening spiritual experiences. These findings affirm the holistic nature of fasting, highlighting its benefits for both mind and spirit.[21]

By integrating the insights of neurotheology into our understanding of fasting, we gain a more comprehensive view of how this practice supports our overall well-being. As we explore the benefits of fasting on brain health, it becomes clear that the effects of fasting extend far beyond the physical body, impacting our mental and emotional states and enriching our spiritual lives.

Exploring the Benefits of Prayer and Fasting on Brain Health

Prayer and fasting are two of the most powerful spiritual disciplines in the Christian tradition, each with distinct yet complementary effects on the brain. When practiced together, these disciplines can lead to profound changes in brain function, enhancing cognitive abilities and promoting emotional and spiritual well-being.

The Neurobiological Effects of Prayer: Prayer is a central practice in the Christian faith, serving as a means of communication with God and a source of spiritual nourishment. From a neurobiological perspective, prayer has been shown to significantly affect brain function, particularly in areas related to attention, emotional regulation, and stress reduction.

Brain Imaging Studies on Prayer: One of the most groundbreaking contributions of neurotheology is the use of brain imaging to study the effects of prayer. Dr. Andrew Newberg's research has shown that regular prayer can lead to changes in brain structure, particularly in the prefrontal cortex and the anterior cingulate cortex—areas of the brain associated with decision-making, emotional regulation, and feelings of compassion. In studies involving fMRI scans, Newberg observed that individuals who engage in regular prayer show increased activity in these regions, suggesting that prayer enhances cognitive function and emotional stability. This increased brain activity is associated with a greater ability to manage stress, maintain focus, and experience a sense of peace and connectedness.

The Role of Prayer in Stress Reduction: Prayer also plays a crucial role in reducing stress and anxiety by modulating the brain's stress response. Newberg's research has shown that prayer can decrease activity in the limbic system, particularly in the amygdala, which is responsible for processing emotions and regulating the body's fight-or-flight response. In *How God Changes Your Brain*, Newberg explains that regular prayer can lower levels of cortisol, the body's primary stress hormone, leading to reduced anxiety and enhanced emotional resilience.[22] This finding aligns with biblical teachings that encourage believers to cast their anxieties on God through prayer, as reflected in 1 Peter 5:7: "Cast all your care upon Him, for He cares for you."

The Neurobiological Effects of Fasting

Fasting, like prayer, has profound effects on the brain, influencing cognitive function, neurogenesis, and emotional well-being. While fasting is often associated with physical health benefits, such as improved metabolism and weight management, it also has significant implications for brain health.

Fasting and Neurogenesis: One of the most exciting findings in neurotheology is the link between fasting and neurogenesis, the process by which new neurons are generated in the brain. Neurogenesis is essential for maintaining cognitive function, learning, and memory, and it can be enhanced by fasting. Research has shown that intermittent fasting increases the production of brain-derived neurotrophic factor (BDNF), a protein that supports the growth and survival of neurons.[23]

BDNF is crucial for neurogenesis and synaptic plasticity—the brain's ability to form and reorganize neural connections in response to new experiences. Increased levels of BDNF are associated with improved cognitive function, memory, and emotional resilience. Additionally, BDNF has a protective effect on the brain, reducing the risk of neurodegenerative diseases such as Alzheimer's and Parkinson's.[24] These findings suggest that fasting can enhance brain health by promoting neurogenesis and protecting against cognitive decline.

Fasting and the Reduction of Inflammation: Fasting has also been shown to reduce inflammation in the brain, which is a key factor in the development of neurodegenerative diseases. Chronic inflammation can lead to the destruction of brain cells and the deterioration of cognitive function, making it essential to find ways to reduce inflammation and protect brain health. A study published in *Nature Medicine* found that fasting triggers the production of anti-inflammatory molecules in the brain, which help reduce inflammation and protect against neurodegeneration.[25]

This reduction in inflammation is particularly important for individuals at risk of developing Alzheimer's disease, as chronic inflammation is a major contributing factor to the progression of the disease.

HOW FASTING AND PRAYER INFLUENCE NEURAL PATHWAYS AND SPIRITUAL EXPERIENCES

The combined effects of fasting and prayer on the brain are profound, influencing not only neural pathways but also the depth and quality of spiritual experiences. When practiced together, fasting and prayer create a powerful synergy that enhances both mental and spiritual well-being. While fasting and prayer each have individual benefits for brain health, their combined effects are even more significant. Fasting creates a state of heightened mental clarity and focus, which enhances the effectiveness of prayer. At the same time, prayer provides spiritual strength and emotional resilience, helping individuals navigate the challenges of fasting.

The Role of Fasting in Enhancing Spiritual Experiences: Fasting has long been used as a means of deepening spiritual experiences and drawing closer to God. By abstaining from food, individuals enter a state of physical and mental purification, which allows them to focus more fully on their spiritual journey. From a neurobiological perspective, fasting enhances spiritual experiences by reducing distractions and increasing mental clarity. Research has shown that fasting increases activity in the prefrontal cortex, the part of the brain responsible for decision-making and self-control. This increased activity helps individuals maintain focus during prayer and meditation, allowing them to connect more deeply with God.[26] These findings suggest that fasting enhances the depth and quality of spiritual experiences, making it a powerful tool for spiritual growth.

The Role of Prayer in Strengthening Neural Pathways That Calm the Brain: Prayer not only enhances spiritual experiences but also strengthens neural pathways in the brain, resulting in calmness and a reduction of anxiety. Research published in *Pastoral Psychology* suggests that prayer has a profound impact on the plasticity and malleability of the human brain. The author makes the case that prayer lowers activity in the amygdala, calming the stress region of the brain. It concludes that the discoveries around plasticity challenge the field of pastoral care and counseling to recognize the ability of contemplative meditational practices like prayer to reduce anxiety as well as facilitate profound changes in the neural pathways of the human brain.[27]

The Neuroplasticity of Spiritual Practices: One of the key insights of neurotheology is the concept of neuroplasticity, the brain's ability to reorganize itself by forming new neural connections throughout life. Neuroplasticity is a critical factor in learning, memory, and the brain's ability to adapt to new experiences. Spiritual practices such as fasting and prayer have been shown to enhance neuroplasticity, promoting the growth of new neural pathways and strengthening existing ones. This process is particularly important for individuals seeking to overcome negative thought patterns or emotional challenges, as it allows the brain to rewire itself in response to positive spiritual experiences.

Research published in *Neuroimage* found that individuals who engaged in regular prayer and meditation showed increased neuroplasticity in the prefrontal cortex and the hippocampus, two areas of the brain associated with cognitive function and emotional regulation.[28] These findings suggest that spiritual practices can lead to lasting changes in the brain, promoting mental and emotional well-being.

INTEGRATING NEUROTHEOLOGY INTO SPIRITUAL PRACTICE

Understanding the insights of neurotheology can enhance our spiritual practice by providing a deeper understanding of how fasting and prayer affect the brain. By recognizing the profound impact these practices have on our mental and spiritual health, we can approach them with greater intentionality and commitment. To integrate the insights of neurotheology into your spiritual practice, consider the following:

- **Combine Fasting with Prayer:** To maximize the benefits of both fasting and prayer, consider practicing them together. The heightened mental clarity and focus achieved through fasting can enhance the effectiveness of prayer, leading to deeper spiritual experiences.[29]
- **Practice Mindfulness During Prayer:** Mindfulness involves paying attention to the present moment with a non-judgmental attitude. By practicing mindfulness during prayer, you can increase your awareness of God's presence and deepen your spiritual connection.[30]
- **Engage in Regular Spiritual Practices:** To promote neuroplasticity and strengthen neural pathways, engage intentionally in regular spiritual practices such as prayer, meditation on the Word. Intentionality in our focus (how we direct our attention) and Consistency are key to achieving lasting changes in the brain and enhancing spiritual growth
- **Seek Opportunities for Spiritual Growth:** Explore new ways to deepen your spiritual practice, such as participating in a retreat, joining a prayer group, or studying Scripture. These

experiences can provide fresh insights and opportunities for growth, further enhancing the benefits of fasting and prayer.

THE HOLISTIC NATURE OF FASTING AND PRAYER

The field of neurotheology offers valuable insights into the intersection of mind, body, and spirit, affirming the profound impact that fasting and prayer have on our brain health and spiritual experiences. By understanding how these practices influence neural pathways and promote spiritual growth, we can approach them with greater intentionality and reverence.[31]

Fasting and prayer are not just isolated practices but are part of a holistic approach to spiritual well-being. By integrating the insights of neurotheology into our spiritual practice, we can enhance our mental, emotional, and spiritual health, leading to a more profound and fulfilling relationship with God.

As we continue to explore the depths of fasting and prayer, let us remember that these practices are gifts from God, designed to nourish our entire being—mind, body, and spirit. By embracing the synergy of faith and science, we can experience the fullness of God's presence in our lives and walk confidently in our spiritual journey.

CHAPTER 14

WHAT ACTUALLY HAPPENS TO YOUR BODY WHEN YOU FAST?

THE TRANSFORMATIVE POWER OF FASTING

While there is a lot of benefit in the spiritual dimension of fasting, it is important to note that this practice goes beyond spiritual discipline; it's a powerful tool that triggers a series of physiological changes within the body. When we fast, our bodies undergo a remarkable transformation, adapting to the absence of food and initiating processes that promote healing, rejuvenation, and overall health. Understanding what happens to your body when you fast can deepen your appreciation for this ancient practice and encourage you to incorporate it into your life with greater intentionality. Knowledge has a powerful way of enlightening and eliciting buy-in.

In this chapter, we will explore the five stages of fasting, detailing the physical changes that occur at each stage, including ketosis, autophagy, and hormone regulation. We'll also examine how the body adapts to extended periods without food, highlighting the profound benefits of fasting for both physical and mental well-being.

The Five Stages of Fasting: A Detailed Exploration

STAGE	DURATION	KEY PROCESSES	PHYSIOLOGICAL BENEFITS
STAGE 1: THE FED STATE	0-4 hours after eating	-Insulin release for glucose uptake -Glycogen storage in liver and muscles -Nutrient absorption	Supports energy supply and initial nutrient processing.
STAGE 2: EARLY FASTING STATE	4-16 hours after eating	-Glycogen breakdown for glucose -Fat mobilization -Decreased insulin levels	Prepares the body for fat metabolism; shifts energy sources from glucose to fat.
STAGE 3: KETOSIS STATE	16-48 hours after eating	-Ketone production from fatty acids -Increased fat burning -Improved mental clarity and focus	Promotes fat burning, mental clarity, and metabolic flexibility.
STAGE 4: DEEP FASTING STATE	48-72 hours after eating	-Enhanced autophagy -Hormone regulation (e.g., HGH) -Immune system reset	Boosts cellular repair, improves immune function, supports metabolic health, and regulates hormones.
STAGE 5: PROLONGED FASTING	72 hours and beyond	-Continued autophagy -Reduction in inflammation -Increased longevity	Provides advanced cellular repair, reduces inflammation, promotes longevity, and supports protection against age-related diseases.

Think of fasting as a dynamic process that unfolds in distinct stages, each characterized by specific physiological changes, more like a metamorphosis. As the body transitions from a fed state to a fasting state, it activates a series of mechanisms designed to conserve energy, protect vital functions, and promote cellular repair. Understanding these stages can provide valuable insights into how fasting benefits the body. It is these changes that are most beneficial to us.

Stage 1: The Fed State (0-4 Hours After Eating)

The first stage of fasting begins immediately after you finish a meal. During this period, the body is in a fed state, actively digesting and absorbing nutrients. Blood glucose levels rise, triggering the release of insulin, a hormone that helps cells take in glucose for energy.[32]

Key Processes During the Fed State:
- **Insulin Release:** Insulin facilitates the uptake of glucose into cells, where it is used for immediate energy or stored as glycogen in the liver and muscles. Excess glucose is converted into fat and stored in adipose tissue.[33]
- **Glycogen Storage:** The liver and muscles store glucose in the form of glycogen, which serves as a quick energy reserve for the body
- **Nutrient Absorption:** Nutrients from the meal, including carbohydrates, proteins, and fats, are absorbed into the bloodstream and distributed to cells for use in various metabolic processes.[34]

The nutrient absorption stage is relatively brief, lasting about four hours after eating. As the body completes the digestion and absorption of nutrients, it transitions into the post-absorptive state, where it begins to tap into stored energy reserves.

Stage 2: The Early Fasting State (4-16 Hours After Eating)

The early fasting state begins approximately four hours after your last meal, as blood glucose levels start to decline, and the body begins to rely on stored glycogen for energy. This stage is often referred to as the post-absorptive state.[35]

Key Processes During the Early Fasting State:
- **Glycogen Breakdown:** The liver breaks down glycogen into glucose, which is released into the bloodstream to maintain stable blood sugar levels.[36]

- **Fat Mobilization:** As glycogen stores become depleted, the body begins to mobilize fat from adipose tissue, breaking it down into fatty acids for energy.[37]
- **Decreased Insulin Levels:** Insulin levels decrease as blood glucose levels drop, signaling the body to shift from using glucose as its primary energy source to using fat.[38]

During this stage, the body is still primarily relying on glucose for energy, but it is beginning to transition to fat metabolism. This stage is crucial for preparing the body for the next phase of fasting, where fat becomes the dominant energy source.

Stage 3: The Ketosis State (16-48 Hours After Eating)

Ketosis is a metabolic state that occurs when the body shifts from using glucose as its primary energy source to using ketones, which are produced from the breakdown of fat. This stage typically begins around sixteen hours after the last meal, though the exact timing can vary depending on factors such as activity level, diet, and individual metabolism.[39]

Key Processes During the Ketosis State:
- **Ketone Production:** As glycogen stores are depleted, the liver begins to convert fatty acids into ketones, which are released into the bloodstream and used as an alternative energy source by the brain and other organs.[40]
- **Increased Fat Burning:** The body increases its reliance on fat for energy, leading to a state of enhanced fat burning. This is one of the key benefits of fasting for weight loss and metabolic health.[41]
- **Mental Clarity and Focus:** Many people report increased mental clarity and focus during ketosis, which is attributed to the steady supply of ketones as a clean, efficient fuel for the brain

The transition to ketosis marks a significant shift in the body's energy metabolism, allowing it to sustain itself during extended periods without food. This stage is often associated with the benefits of intermittent fasting and ketogenic diets, which aim to maintain the body in a state of ketosis for prolonged periods.

Stage 4: The Deep Fasting State (48-72 Hours After Eating)

The deep fasting state occurs when the body has been without food for forty-eight to seventy-two hours. During this stage, the body is fully adapted to fasting, relying almost exclusively on fat and ketones for energy. This state is characterized by a number of beneficial physiological processes, including enhanced autophagy and hormone regulation.

Key Processes During the Deep Fasting State:

- **Enhanced Autophagy:** Autophagy, the body's cellular cleanup process, is significantly upregulated during deep fasting. This process involves the breakdown of damaged cells and proteins, which are recycled and used to support vital functions. Autophagy plays a critical role in preventing the accumulation of cellular waste that can lead to diseases such as cancer and neurodegenerative disorders.[42]
- **Hormone Regulation:** Fasting triggers the release of several important hormones, including human growth hormone (HGH), which supports tissue repair and muscle preservation. Additionally, fasting helps regulate insulin and leptin levels, improving insulin sensitivity and promoting satiety.[43]
- **Immune System Reset:** Extended fasting has been shown to promote the regeneration of immune cells, leading to a "reset" of the immune system. This process is thought to enhance the

body's ability to fight infections and may have implications for autoimmune diseases.[44]

The deep fasting state is where many of the long-term health benefits of fasting begin to manifest. This stage is associated with improved metabolic health, enhanced immune function, and increased longevity.

Stage 5: The Prolonged Fasting State (72 Hours and Beyond)

The prolonged fasting state occurs after seventy-two hours of fasting. At this stage, the body has fully adapted to the absence of food, relying on fat stores and ketones for energy. Prolonged fasting is associated with a number of therapeutic benefits, including enhanced cellular repair, reduced inflammation, and improved metabolic health.

Key Processes During the Prolonged Fasting State:

- **Continued Autophagy:** Autophagy continues to be upregulated during prolonged fasting, promoting cellular repair and the removal of damaged cells. This process is particularly beneficial for preventing age-related diseases and supporting overall health.[45]
- **Reduction in Inflammation:** Prolonged fasting has been shown to reduce levels of inflammatory markers in the body, which can help protect against chronic diseases such as heart disease, diabetes, and cancer.[46]
- **Increased Longevity:** Research on prolonged fasting suggests that it may promote longevity by enhancing cellular repair, reducing oxidative stress, and improving metabolic function. Studies on animals have shown that prolonged fasting can extend lifespan, and emerging research suggests that similar benefits may apply to humans.[47]

While prolonged fasting offers significant health benefits, it is important to approach this practice with caution, particularly for individuals with underlying health conditions. Consulting with a healthcare professional before embarking on an extended fast is recommended.

PHYSICAL CHANGES DURING FASTING: KETOSIS, AUTOPHAGY, AND HORMONE REGULATION

As the body progresses through the stages of fasting, it undergoes a series of physical changes that support health and well-being. These changes include the induction of ketosis, the activation of autophagy, and the regulation of hormones, all of which contribute to the benefits of fasting.

Ketosis: The Metabolic Shift to Fat Burning

Ketosis is a metabolic state in which the body shifts from using glucose as its primary energy source to using ketones, which are produced from the breakdown of fat. This shift occurs when glycogen stores are depleted, typically around sixteen to forty-eight hours after the last meal.

The Benefits of Ketosis:
- **Enhanced Fat Burning:** Ketosis increases the body's reliance on fat for energy, leading to enhanced fat burning and weight loss. This is one of the key benefits of fasting for individuals seeking to lose weight or improve metabolic health.
- **Improved Mental Clarity:** Many people report improved mental clarity and focus during ketosis, which is attributed to the steady supply of ketones as a clean, efficient fuel for the brain.

- **Reduced Risk of Chronic Diseases:** Ketosis has been shown to improve metabolic markers, such as blood sugar levels and insulin sensitivity, which can reduce the risk of chronic diseases such as type 2 diabetes and cardiovascular disease.[48]

Autophagy: The Body's Cellular Cleanup Process

Autophagy is a process by which the body breaks down and recycles damaged cells and proteins. This process is upregulated during fasting, particularly during the deep fasting and prolonged fasting stages.

The Benefits of Autophagy:

- **Cellular Repair:** Autophagy promotes the removal of damaged cells and proteins, supporting cellular repair and regeneration. This process is critical for preventing the accumulation of cellular waste that can lead to diseases such as cancer and neurodegenerative disorders.[49]
- **Disease Prevention:** By clearing out damaged cells and proteins, autophagy helps prevent the development of chronic diseases, including cancer, Alzheimer's disease, and Parkinson's disease.
- **Increased Longevity:** Enhanced autophagy is associated with increased longevity, as it supports the maintenance of healthy cells and tissues, reducing the risk of age-related diseases.[50]

Hormone Regulation: Balancing Key Hormones

Fasting has a profound impact on hormone regulation, influencing the levels of several key hormones that play a critical role in metabolism, appetite, and overall health.

Key Hormones Affected by Fasting:

- **Insulin:** Fasting reduces insulin levels, which helps improve insulin sensitivity and lower blood sugar levels. This effect is

particularly beneficial for individuals with insulin resistance or type 2 diabetes.
- **Human Growth Hormone (HGH):** Fasting increases the release of HGH, a hormone that supports tissue repair, muscle preservation, and fat metabolism. Elevated HGH levels during fasting help protect lean muscle mass while promoting fat loss.[51]
- **Leptin and Ghrelin:** Fasting influences the levels of leptin and ghrelin, hormones that regulate hunger and satiety. Leptin levels increase during fasting, promoting feelings of fullness, while ghrelin levels decrease, reducing hunger. This hormonal balance helps individuals manage their appetite and maintain a healthy weight.

HOW THE BODY ADAPTS TO EXTENDED PERIODS WITHOUT FOOD

The human body is remarkably adaptable, capable of sustaining itself during extended periods without food through a series of physiological changes. These adaptations allow the body to conserve energy, protect vital functions, and promote health and longevity.

Metabolic Adaptations:
- **Energy Conservation:** During extended fasting, the body conserves energy by reducing metabolic rate and prioritizing essential functions. This energy conservation helps the body survive prolonged periods without food.
- **Fat Utilization:** As glycogen stores are depleted, the body shifts to using fat as its primary energy source. This shift to fat utilization is a key adaptation that allows the body to sustain itself during extended fasting.

- **Ketone Production:** The liver increases the production of ketones, which serve as an alternative energy source for the brain and other organs. Ketones are a more efficient fuel than glucose, providing a steady supply of energy during fasting.

Cellular Adaptations:

- **Enhanced Autophagy:** As discussed earlier, autophagy is upregulated during fasting, promoting the removal of damaged cells and the regeneration of healthy ones. This cellular adaptation helps protect the body from disease and supports overall health.
- **Immune System Support:** Extended fasting promotes the regeneration of immune cells, leading to a "reset" of the immune system. This adaptation enhances the body's ability to fight infections and may have therapeutic implications for autoimmune diseases.[52]

THE POWER OF FASTING FOR HEALTH AND WELL-BEING

Fasting is a powerful practice that triggers a series of physiological changes, promoting health and well-being on multiple levels. By understanding what happens to your body when you fast, you can appreciate the profound benefits of this ancient discipline and approach it with greater intentionality.

As you consider incorporating fasting into your life, remember that the body's ability to adapt to fasting is a testament to its resilience and capacity for self-healing. Whether you are fasting for spiritual reasons, health benefits, or both, you can be confident that your body is equipped to thrive during extended periods without food, thanks to the remarkable processes of ketosis, autophagy, and hormone regulation.

What Actually Happens to Your Body When You Fast? 147

Be empowered as you embrace fasting as a transformative practice that supports your overall health and well-being, allowing you to experience the fullness of life—body, mind, and spirit.

CHAPTER 15

COMMON SYMPTOMS WHILE FASTING

SHIFTING YOUR MINDSET: FASTING AS A GAIN, NOT A LOSS

Perspective saves lives, and context is king. While some view fasting as losing, a more powerful perspective is to view fasting as a gain rather than a loss. By focusing on what you are gaining—spiritual clarity, deeper connection with God, and even physical renewal—fasting becomes less about deprivation and more about transformation. This mindset shift is crucial for overcoming the physical discomforts that often accompany fasting.

In this chapter, we will explore the essence of fasting from this transformative perspective, address common physical symptoms like headaches, hunger, and fatigue, and offer practical tips for managing these challenges. We will also delve into the spiritual significance of enduring physical discomfort during fasting, which can become a powerful tool for spiritual growth.

Mindset Shift: The Essence of Fasting

Fasting is more than just abstaining from food or other pleasures; it is a journey toward spiritual and physical renewal. When you focus on what you are gaining—spiritual insights, heightened awareness of God's presence, and a purified body—you can transform the experience of fasting from one of deprivation to one of abundance.

1) **Gaining Spiritual Clarity**

One of the most profound gains of fasting is spiritual clarity. By removing distractions and focusing on your relationship with God, fasting allows you to hear His voice more clearly and understand His will for your life. This clarity often comes through prayer, meditation, and time spent in God's Word, all of which are amplified during a fast.

2) **Deepening Your Connection with God**

Fasting is a powerful way to draw closer to God. It is a time to seek His presence, to listen for His guidance, and to experience His peace more deeply. As you set aside the physical and focus on the spiritual, your relationship with God can grow more intimate, leading to greater spiritual maturity.

3) **Physical Renewal**

From a physical standpoint, fasting offers the body a chance to reset and renew. The physiological processes that occur during fasting, such as detoxification and autophagy, promote healing and regeneration at the cellular level. This renewal is not just physical but can also be a metaphor for the spiritual renewal that occurs during a fast.

By shifting your focus to these gains, the physical discomforts of fasting become more manageable, and the entire experience is enriched.

ADDRESSING COMMON PHYSICAL DISCOMFORT SYMPTOMS DURING FASTING

Despite the benefits, fasting often comes with physical challenges. Symptoms such as headaches, hunger, and fatigue are common, especially in the early stages. Understanding these symptoms and knowing how to manage them can help you maintain a positive mindset and stay focused on your spiritual gains.

Headaches

Headaches are a frequent complaint during fasting, particularly in the first few days. They can range from mild to severe but are usually temporary.

Causes of Headaches During Fasting:
- **Dehydration:** Often, headaches are a result of not drinking enough water. As food intake decreases, it's easy to forget to stay hydrated, which can lead to dehydration.
- **Caffeine withdrawal:** If you're accustomed to consuming caffeine, fasting can lead to withdrawal symptoms, including headaches, as your body adjusts to the lack of caffeine.
- **Blood sugar fluctuations:** Fasting causes a drop in blood sugar levels, which can trigger headaches, particularly if your body is used to frequent meals.

Practical Tips for Managing Headaches:
- **Stay hydrated:** Drink plenty of water throughout your fast. Herbal teas or water infused with electrolytes can also help.
- **Reduce caffeine gradually:** Before starting your fast, gradually reduce your caffeine intake to minimize withdrawal symptoms.

- **Rest and relaxation:** If you experience a headache, take time to rest. Gentle stretching, deep breathing, or a short walk can also help alleviate tension.

Hunger

Hunger is a natural response during fasting, particularly in the beginning. Your body is accustomed to regular food intake, and when this is interrupted, hunger signals can become more intense.

Causes of Hunger During Fasting:
- **Ghrelin hormone:** Ghrelin, the hormone responsible for hunger, signals the brain when it's time to eat. During fasting, ghrelin levels can spike, leading to increased hunger pangs.
- **Habitual eating:** Your body's internal clock may trigger hunger at regular mealtimes, even if you're not physically in need of food.

Practical Tips for Managing Hunger:
- **Hydrate:** Drinking water can help fill your stomach and reduce hunger sensations. Herbal teas or broths can also be comforting.
- **Stay occupied:** Engage in activities that take your mind off food, such as reading, praying, or walking. If you are working, take the lunch hour break and pray or read your Bible. Don't be idle. The more you ignore the hunger pangs, the more the levels of ghrelin go down, and you return back to normal function.
- **Embrace the hunger:** View hunger as a temporary sensation and a reminder of your spiritual goals during the fast. Remember, it's more about what you're gaining than what you're giving up. This switch of focus will go a long way in providing perspective and strength.

Fatigue

Fatigue is another common symptom during fasting. It can manifest as physical tiredness, mental fog, or a general lack of energy, especially in the early stages. This does not mean that anything is wrong or it's time to panic and reach for the nearest cookie. It's all a core part of the beneficial journey of fasting.

Causes of Fatigue During Fasting:
- **Glycogen depletion:** The body uses up its glycogen stores early in fasting, leading to a temporary drop in energy.
- **Ketosis transition:** As the body transitions from using glucose to using ketones for energy, there may be a period of low energy.
- **Reduced caloric intake:** Naturally, fewer calories during fasting can lead to lower energy levels.

Practical Tips for Managing Fatigue:
- **Rest:** Give yourself permission to rest more during your fast. This is a time for slowing down and focusing on spiritual renewal.
- **Gentle activity:** Engage in gentle activities like walking, stretching, or yoga to boost energy and circulation.
- **Electrolyte balance:** Ensure you are staying hydrated and consider adding electrolytes to your water to maintain energy levels.

THE SPIRITUAL SIGNIFICANCE OF ENDURING PHYSICAL DISCOMFORT DURING FASTING

Physical discomfort during fasting is not merely something to be endured; it is an integral part of the spiritual journey. These discomforts can become opportunities for spiritual growth, helping you to deepen your faith and reliance on God.

Embracing Sacrifice as Spiritual Discipline

Fasting is a form of self-denial that mirrors the sacrifices made by biblical figures in their pursuit of spiritual breakthroughs. By enduring the physical discomforts of fasting, you participate in a tradition of sacrifice that has been a powerful tool for spiritual growth throughout history.

In Matthew 4:1-2, we see Jesus fasting for forty days and nights, enduring hunger and physical weakness as He prepared for His ministry. His fast was a time of spiritual preparation and a demonstration of His complete reliance on God. Similarly, your fast is an opportunity to sacrifice the comforts of food and depend more fully on God's strength.

1) Building Spiritual Resilience

Fasting challenges both the body and the spirit. By pushing through physical discomfort, you build spiritual resilience—an essential quality for enduring life's challenges. This resilience is about learning to trust in God's provision and power, even when your physical body feels weak. James 1:2-4 encourages us to "count it all joy when you fall into various trials, knowing that the testing of your faith produces patience." Fasting provides an opportunity to exercise this patience and endurance, helping you to develop a stronger, more resilient faith.

2) Deepening Dependence on God

Physical discomfort during fasting serves as a powerful reminder of your dependence on God. As your body experiences hunger or fatigue, it's an opportunity to turn your focus to God, seeking His presence and sustenance. In Matthew 4:4, Jesus reminds us, "Man shall not live by bread alone, but by every word that proceeds from the mouth of God." Fasting brings this truth into sharp focus, as you experience firsthand the limitations of physical sustenance and the boundless sufficiency of God's Word.

3) **Transforming Discomfort into Spiritual Growth**

The physical discomforts of fasting—headaches, hunger, and fatigue—are real, but they are also temporary and manageable. More importantly, these challenges offer opportunities for spiritual growth and deeper reliance on God. By shifting your mindset to focus on the gains of fasting rather than the losses, and by employing practical strategies to manage physical symptoms, you can navigate your fasting journey with greater ease and purpose. Embrace the discomforts as part of the process, knowing that each moment of physical challenge is a step toward greater spiritual growth.

May you find strength in God's presence and grow in your faith as you continue your fasting journey, transforming each challenge into an opportunity for deeper spiritual renewal.

PART 3

Embracing the Lifestyle of Fasting

THE ONGOING JOURNEY OF FASTING

As we delve deeper into the spiritual discipline of fasting, it's important to recognize that fasting is more than just a temporary practice or a response to specific needs—it's a lifestyle. Embracing fasting as a regular part of your spiritual routine can lead to sustained growth, renewal, and a deeper relationship with God. When fasting becomes a lifestyle, it transforms from an occasional discipline into a powerful rhythm that aligns your heart and mind with the purposes of God.

Incorporating fasting into your life brings with it profound benefits, both spiritually and physically. By making fasting a regular practice, you create a space in your life for ongoing spiritual renewal and intimacy with God. This discipline not only sharpens your spiritual focus but also promotes physical health, as intermittent fasting has been shown to support overall well-being. The lifestyle of fasting becomes a powerful tool for maintaining a healthy balance between body and spirit, leading to holistic transformation.

But fasting is not a journey you must undertake alone. The power of community in fasting is immense. When believers come together to fast, there is a multiplication of spiritual power and support. Accountability and encouragement from others strengthen your resolve and deepen your spiritual experience. Fasting within a community enhances not only individual spirituality but also collective faith, drawing the entire community closer to God. The shared experience of fasting creates bonds of unity and empowers communities to seek God together with greater fervor and purpose.

Fasting also plays a critical role in spiritual warfare. It is a powerful weapon that can break strongholds and bring deliverance in the midst of spiritual battles. Throughout Scripture, fasting has been used to seek God's intervention and breakthrough in times of crisis. By integrating fasting into your spiritual arsenal, you equip yourself with a potent tool to overcome challenges, resist temptation, and stand firm in your faith. The discipline of fasting prepares you to engage in spiritual warfare with renewed strength and divine authority.

Moreover, fasting has the potential to spark personal and communal revival. Throughout history, we see that periods of fasting have often preceded powerful moves of God, leading to transformation and renewal. Fasting invites the presence of God in a profound way, making it a catalyst for revival. As you engage in fasting, you open the door for God to bring about significant change in your life and in the lives of those around you. Whether you are seeking personal breakthrough or interceding for your community, fasting can ignite a revival that impacts both the spiritual and physical realms.

As you continue this journey, you may have questions about fasting—whether you're new to the practice or have been fasting for years. It's important to seek out wisdom and clarity, address any misconceptions, and gain practical insights that can help you navigate the path ahead. Fasting is a journey of discovery, and as you grow in this discipline, you will find answers that deepen your understanding and enhance your experience.

In this next phase of the book, you are invited to fully embrace the lifestyle of fasting. This is a journey of continual spiritual growth, renewal, and empowerment. As you integrate fasting into your daily life, you will discover its profound impact on your relationship with God and its power to bring about lasting change. Stay engaged, keep your heart open, and allow fasting to become a cornerstone of your spiritual life, leading you into deeper intimacy with God and greater spiritual maturity.

The road ahead is rich with potential for personal and communal transformation. Embrace this lifestyle of fasting with expectancy, knowing that it is not just a discipline, but a divine invitation to live in closer alignment with the heart of God.

CHAPTER 16

FASTING AS A LIFESTYLE

EMBRACING FASTING AS A WAY OF LIFE

Fasting, when embraced as a lifestyle, transcends the boundaries of an occasional spiritual discipline and becomes a continuous source of spiritual and physical renewal. It's not just about setting aside time for a single fast during a season of need, but about integrating fasting into the very fabric of your spiritual routine. By doing so, you create a rhythm that aligns you more closely with God's will, allows for ongoing purification, and fosters spiritual growth. The Bible presents fasting as a powerful tool used by believers throughout history to seek God, gain clarity, and experience breakthrough. When we incorporate fasting into our lives regularly, we open ourselves up to these same benefits, allowing God to work in us continually. This chapter explores how to make fasting a consistent part of your spiritual routine, the benefits of intermittent fasting, and how to live a life marked by periodic fasting and spiritual renewal.

Making fasting a regular part of your spiritual routine requires intentionality and commitment. It's about establishing a pattern of seeking God through fasting, not just in times of crisis or special need, but as an ongoing practice that strengthens your relationship with Him.

Setting Regular Fasting Days

One of the most effective ways to incorporate fasting into your life is by setting regular fasting days. For example, you might choose to fast one day a week or several days each month. These scheduled fasts serve as intentional times to draw closer to God, pray, and meditate on His Word. In the New Testament, the early church practiced regular fasting as a means of spiritual discipline and seeking God's guidance. In Acts 13:2-3, we read, "As they ministered to the Lord and fasted, the Holy Spirit said, 'Now separate to Me Barnabas and Saul for the work to which I have called them.' Then, having fasted and prayed, and laid hands on them, they sent *them* away." This passage highlights the importance of regular fasting in the life of the early believers as they sought direction from God. By establishing a routine of fasting, you cultivate a lifestyle of dependence on God, continually positioning yourself to hear His voice and align with His will.

Pairing Fasting with Prayer and Scripture Study

Fasting should always be accompanied by prayer and Scripture study. The purpose of fasting is not merely to abstain from food but to devote the time you would normally spend eating to spiritual pursuits. This is a time to deepen your understanding of God's Word and to seek His presence more fervently. Jesus Himself demonstrated the importance of pairing fasting with prayer and the Word of God. During His forty days of fasting in the wilderness, Jesus responded to Satan's temptations by quoting Scripture, saying, "It is written, 'Man shall not live by bread alone, but by every word that proceeds from the mouth of God'" (Matthew 4:4). This shows us that fasting is most powerful when it is rooted in prayer and the truth of God's Word. As you fast, set aside time each day to pray, meditate on Scripture, and listen for God's guidance. This practice will not only sustain you during the fast but will also lead to greater spiritual insight and growth.

THE BENEFITS OF INTERMITTENT FASTING FOR ONGOING SPIRITUAL AND PHYSICAL HEALTH

Intermittent fasting, a practice that involves regular periods of fasting followed by periods of eating, has gained popularity not only for its spiritual benefits but also for its positive effects on physical health. This approach to fasting can be easily incorporated into your lifestyle, providing ongoing opportunities for spiritual renewal while also promoting physical well-being. Intermittent fasting creates a consistent rhythm of drawing near to God. By regularly setting aside time to fast, you continually remind yourself of your dependence on Him and create space for spiritual renewal. This practice can lead to:

- **Increased spiritual sensitivity:** Regular fasting helps to sharpen your spiritual senses, making you more attuned to the leading of the Holy Spirit. As you deny the flesh, you heighten your awareness of the spiritual realm, making it easier to hear God's voice and discern His will.
- **Ongoing repentance and purification:** Fasting provides regular opportunities for self-examination and repentance. In Psalm 51:17, David writes, "The sacrifices of God are a broken spirit, a broken and a contrite heart—These, O God, You will not despise." Intermittent fasting helps to cultivate a heart of humility and repentance, keeping you in right relationship with God.

- **Continual spiritual growth:** By making fasting a regular practice, you create an environment for ongoing spiritual growth. Fasting becomes a time of dedicated focus on God, allowing you to grow in your faith, understanding, and obedience to His Word.

Physical Benefits of Intermittent Fasting

In addition to its spiritual benefits, intermittent fasting also has significant positive effects on physical health. Research has shown that intermittent fasting can lead to:

- **Improved metabolic health:** Regular fasting periods can help regulate blood sugar levels, improve insulin sensitivity, and promote weight loss. This is particularly beneficial for maintaining a healthy metabolism and reducing the risk of chronic diseases such as diabetes.
- **Cellular repair and detoxification:** Fasting triggers autophagy, a process by which the body cleans out damaged cells and regenerates new ones. This cellular repair process helps to prevent disease, reduce inflammation, and promote overall health.
- **Enhanced mental clarity:** Many people report increased mental clarity and focus during intermittent fasting. By giving your body a break from constant digestion, you allow more energy to be directed towards brain function, leading to improved cognitive performance.

HOW TO LIVE A LIFE MARKED BY PERIODIC FASTING AND SPIRITUAL RENEWAL

Living a life marked by periodic fasting and spiritual renewal means integrating fasting into your life as a regular and intentional practice.

This requires discipline, but the rewards are immense—both spiritually and physically.

Begin by developing a fasting routine that works for your lifestyle and spiritual goals. Whether it's weekly, monthly, or quarterly, choose specific days to fast and commit to them. As you establish this routine, you'll find that fasting becomes a natural part of your spiritual rhythm, helping you to stay connected with God and aligned with His will. Approach each fast with a specific purpose in mind—whether it's to seek God's guidance, intercede for others, or simply draw closer to Him. As you fast, focus on this purpose and allow God to speak to you and work in your life. Fasting with intention leads to deeper spiritual experiences and greater breakthroughs.

In Joel 2:12-13, God calls His people to return to Him with fasting, saying:

Now, therefore, says the LORD, "Turn to Me with all your heart, with fasting, with weeping, and with mourning." So rend your heart, and not your garments; return to the LORD your God, for He is gracious and merciful, slow to anger, and of great kindness.

This passage reminds us that fasting is a way of returning to God with our whole heart, seeking His grace and mercy. After each fast, take time to reflect on what God has shown you and how you can apply it to your daily life. Maintain the spiritual insights and physical benefits gained during the fast by continuing in prayer, Scripture study, and healthy living. Periodic fasting, when coupled with consistent devotion, leads to sustained spiritual growth and renewal.

As we conclude this chapter, remember that fasting as a lifestyle is an ongoing journey of spiritual and physical renewal. By incorporating fasting into your regular spiritual routine, you create a rhythm of seeking God that brings continual growth and transformation. Intermittent fasting offers a practical way to maintain this discipline, providing both spiritual and physical benefits that enhance your overall well-being. As you embrace fasting as a way of life, you will find that it becomes a powerful tool for drawing closer to God, purifying your heart, and aligning your life with His purposes. Fasting is not just a practice for special occasions; it is a discipline that, when integrated into your daily walk with God, brings lasting change and deepening intimacy with the Lord.

CHAPTER 17

THE POWER OF COMMUNITY IN FASTING

THE STRENGTH FOUND IN FASTING TOGETHER

Fasting is traditionally seen as a personal spiritual discipline, a time for individual believers to draw nearer to God through self-denial and focused prayer. However, throughout both Scripture and church history, fasting is also recognized as a powerful communal practice. When believers unite in fasting, the spiritual power of their collective sacrifice and prayer can lead to remarkable divine interventions, spiritual breakthroughs, and even societal change. The strength of fasting together lies in the shared commitment to seek God's face, to support one another in spiritual discipline, and to amplify the impact of individual prayers through the unity of the body of Christ. This chapter will explore the essential role of accountability and support in a successful fast, how fasting within a community strengthens both individual and collective spirituality, and provide historical case studies that illustrate the profound impact of communal fasts in both biblical times and throughout church history.

The Role of Accountability and Support in a Successful Fast

When we fast within a community, accountability and support become vital components of the spiritual experience. The collective effort helps ensure that each individual remains committed to the fast, providing encouragement during moments of weakness and fostering a deeper connection with one another and with God.

The Bible teaches us the value of accountability in our spiritual walk. Ecclesiastes 4:9-10 reminds us that "Two *are* better than one, because they have a good reward for their labor. For if they fall, one will lift up his companion. But woe to him *who is* alone when he falls, for *he has* no one to help him up." Fasting with others helps us stay accountable to our commitments, knowing that we are not alone in our journey.

In a community fast, participants often share their goals, struggles, and victories with one another, creating a network of support that strengthens resolve. Whether through group meetings, prayer circles, or simply checking in with a fasting partner, the communal aspect of fasting ensures that each person is encouraged to persevere, even when the fast becomes challenging.

Support in communal fasting extends beyond mere accountability; it involves active participation in each other's spiritual journey. When a group fasts together, they pray for one another, lift up individual needs, and seek collective breakthrough. James 5:16 emphasizes the power of such communal prayer: "Confess *your* trespasses to one another, and pray for one another, that you may be healed. The effective, fervent prayer of a righteous man avails much."

This mutual support not only enhances the fasting experience but also deepens the bonds between participants, fostering a sense of spiritual unity that reflects the communal nature of the early church.

Fasting within a community amplifies the spiritual impact of the practice. While individual fasting draws a person closer to God, communal fasting unites believers in a shared purpose, creating a powerful spiritual synergy that can lead to both personal and collective transformation.

Strengthening Individual Spirituality Through Communal Fasting

When fasting is done within a community, each participant benefits from the collective focus on God. The knowledge that others are fasting with you provides a sense of solidarity and encouragement, making it easier to stay committed and to go deeper in your spiritual walk.

The early church provides a clear example of this in Acts 13:2-3: "As they ministered to the Lord and fasted, the Holy Spirit said, 'Now separate to Me Barnabas and Saul for the work to which I have called them.' Then, having fasted and prayed, and laid hands on them, they sent *them* away." The communal fasting and prayer led to divine direction and the empowerment of individuals for ministry, illustrating how collective fasting can strengthen individual callings and spiritual clarity.

Strengthening Collective Spirituality and Unity

Fasting together as a community not only strengthens individual believers but also enhances the spiritual unity of the group. Joel 2:15-16 captures this concept:

> *Blow the trumpet in Zion,*
> *Consecrate a fast,*
> *Call a sacred assembly;*

> *Gather the people,*
> *Sanctify the congregation,*
> *Assemble the elders,*
> *Gather the children and nursing babes;*
> *Let the bridegroom go out from his chamber,*
> *And the bride from her dressing room.*

Here, the entire community is called to fast together, highlighting the importance of collective repentance and seeking God as a unified body.

This unity in fasting can lead to profound spiritual renewal within a community, as members support one another in their shared pursuit of God's presence and guidance.

The Role of Fasting and Prayer in Church History

Throughout the history of the Christian church, periods of intense prayer and fasting have often been catalysts for significant spiritual movements and revivals. These practices, deeply rooted in both personal piety and communal devotion, have consistently demonstrated their power to shape not only the spiritual lives of individuals but also the course of entire nations. The following profiles highlight key revivals and movements where prayer and fasting played a pivotal role in bringing about profound change.

1) **The Revival at Antioch (Acts 13)**

Biblical history also provides a compelling example of how fasting can change the course of church history. In Acts 13, we see the leaders of the church in Antioch fasting and praying when the Holy Spirit directed them to set apart Paul and Barnabas for missionary work. This moment of fasting and prayer led to the first major missionary journey in Christian history, resulting in the spread of the gospel across the Roman Empire and the eventual writing of many New Testament books by Paul. The impact of this revival cannot be overstated, as it laid the foundation for the global church.

2) **The Businessmen's Revival (1857-1858)**

The Businessmen's Revival, also known as the Layman's Prayer Revival, began in New York City in 1857 and was initiated by Jeremiah Lanphier, a layman who started a weekly prayer meeting. What began as a small gathering grew into a massive movement, with daily prayer meetings held across the city. Fasting was a common practice among those who participated, as they sought God for personal and national revival during a time of economic hardship.

This revival led to an estimated one million conversions across the United States. The revival's impact was not limited to America; it spread to other parts of the world, including the British Isles, where another million people were converted. The Businessmen's Revival illustrates the power of united prayer and fasting in bringing about spiritual renewal on a global scale.

3) **The Methodist Revival with John Wesley**

John Wesley, a central figure in the Methodist Revival of the eighteenth century, was a staunch advocate of regular fasting and prayer as essential disciplines for spiritual growth and renewal. Wesley practiced fasting twice a week and encouraged his followers to do the same. This discipline was not merely a personal habit but a communal practice that underpinned the Methodist movement.

The revival, characterized by an emphasis on holiness, social justice, and evangelism, was fueled by these disciplines. Wesley's methodical approach, which included structured times of fasting, fostered a deeply committed community that was fervent in its spiritual pursuits.

The outcomes of the Methodist Revival were far-reaching, leading to the revitalization of the Church of England and the establishment of the Methodist Church, which remains influential worldwide.

4) The Welsh Revival (1904-1905)

The Welsh Revival, led by Evan Roberts, is one of the most remarkable examples of how collective fasting and prayer can lead to widespread spiritual awakening. Beginning in 1904, the revival was marked by intense prayer meetings where fasting was a common practice. The movement led to the conversion of thousands, significant social reforms, and a deep moral and spiritual renewal in Wales.

Robert Liardon, a renowned church historian, notes that the Welsh Revival was a direct result of fervent prayer and fasting, which prepared the hearts of the people for a powerful move of God. The revival's impact was so profound that it spread beyond Wales, influencing global Christian movements, including the Azusa Street Revival in Los Angeles.[53]

5) The National Day of Prayer Called by King George VI (1940)

In 1940, facing the dire threat of Nazi invasion during World War II, King George VI called for a National Day of Prayer and Fasting. The British people responded overwhelmingly, filling churches across the nation to seek divine intervention. This collective act of humility and dependence on God was followed by what many consider the "Miracle of Dunkirk," where nearly 338,000 Allied soldiers were evacuated from the beaches of Dunkirk against overwhelming odds.

This event underscores the power of united prayer and fasting in shaping the course of history. It serves as a powerful reminder of how a nation's collective cry to God can lead to extraordinary outcomes, even in the face of seemingly insurmountable challenges.

6) The Great Awakenings in America

The Great Awakenings were periods of religious revival that swept through the American colonies in the eighteenth and nineteenth centuries. These movements were characterized by a renewed emphasis on personal repentance, holiness, and a deep commitment to God. Central to these revivals was the practice of fasting and prayer, which leaders like Jonathan Edwards and Charles Finney championed as essential for spiritual breakthrough.

Robert Liardon highlights how Charles Finney, known as the father of modern revivalism, often employed fasting and prayer as preparatory tools for his revival meetings. Finney's success was partly due to the dedicated prayer warriors, such as Father Nash, who would fast and pray intensely before Finney's meetings, creating a spiritual atmosphere ripe for revival.[54] The impact of the Great Awakenings was profound, leading to widespread conversions, the establishment of new denominations, and significant social reforms, including the abolition of slavery.

7) The Azusa Street Revival (1906-1915)

The Azusa Street Revival in Los Angeles, led by William J. Seymour, is another significant example of the power of communal fasting and prayer. This revival, which birthed the modern Pentecostal movement, was characterized by continuous prayer and fasting, seeking a fresh outpouring of the Holy Spirit. The revival broke down racial and social barriers, bringing together people from diverse backgrounds in a powerful display of unity and spiritual fervor.

Liardon's research into this revival emphasizes how fasting and prayer were integral to sustaining the movement and creating an environment where miracles, healings, and other spiritual gifts were regularly experienced.[55] The Azusa Street Revival's influence continues to be felt worldwide, as it laid the foundation for the growth of Pentecostalism, now one of the largest Christian movements globally.

THE ROLE OF FASTING IN CONTEMPORARY MOVEMENTS: MODERN-DAY REVIVALS AND THE ROLE OF FASTING

In modern times, consecration disciplines like fasting and prayer continue to play a vital role in spiritual awakenings and revivals. The role of fasting in revivals like the Jesus Movement of the 1960s and the Brownsville Revival in the 1990s were marked by periods of intense fasting and prayer. These modern-day movements saw a renewed emphasis on holiness, evangelism, and social justice, all underpinned by a commitment to fasting as a means of seeking God's guidance and power.

Revival patterns have also shown that in times of spiritual decline, churches that emphasize fasting and prayer often experience renewal and growth.

The historical and modern examples presented here clearly demonstrate that fasting is a powerful tool for those who desire to see God move in mighty ways. Whether you are seeking personal breakthrough, revival in your church, or transformation in your community, fasting can position you to experience the fullness of God's power and presence.

Fasting is not merely a ritual; it is an act of faith, a demonstration of our hunger for God's intervention. As you commit to fasting, remember the promises of Scripture: "If my people who are called by My name will humble themselves, and pray and seek My face, and turn from their wicked ways, then I will hear from heaven, and will forgive their sin and will heal their land" (2 Chronicles 7:14).

These historical examples illustrate the transformative power of prayer and fasting in shaping the course of church history. Whether through the disciplined practices of John Wesley, the fervent prayers of the Welsh Revival, or the national cry for deliverance during World War II, fasting and prayer have been powerful tools that God has used to bring about spiritual awakening, societal change, and divine intervention. As Roberts Liardon's works reveal, these practices are not just historical footnotes but timeless principles that continue to hold relevance for the church today. The legacy of these revivals reminds us that when God's people humble themselves, fast, and pray, they can expect to see His hand move powerfully in their midst.

CHAPTER 18

FASTING AND SPIRITUAL WARFARE

THE POWER OF FASTING IN SPIRITUAL WARFARE

Fasting is a spiritual discipline with the power to break strongholds, overcome the enemy, and secure divine intervention. It is a weapon that sharpens our spiritual senses and aligns us with God's will, making us more effective in spiritual warfare. Throughout the Bible, fasting is often coupled with prayer as a means to humble oneself before God, seek His guidance, and gain victory in spiritual battles. This chapter delves into the role of fasting in overcoming spiritual challenges, examining scriptural examples of fasting for deliverance and breakthrough, and offering practical steps to use fasting effectively in spiritual warfare.

The Bible teaches that believers are engaged in a spiritual battle not against flesh and blood, but against principalities, powers, and spiritual forces of wickedness (Ephesians 6:12). Fasting plays a crucial role in this battle by weakening the flesh, enhancing spiritual clarity, and drawing us closer to God. Through fasting, believers can more effectively resist the enemy, stand firm in their faith, and invoke divine intervention. Fasting allows us to deny our fleshly desires, focusing our energy and attention on spiritual matters. By doing so, we become more sensitive to the Holy Spirit's guidance, enabling us to discern the enemy's tactics and stand firm against them. The act of fasting, coupled with fervent prayer, serves as a spiritual reset that fortifies our faith and empowers us to engage in spiritual warfare with renewed strength and determination.

Fasting for Deliverance and Breakthrough

The Bible provides numerous examples of fasting being used to secure deliverance, victory, and divine intervention in times of crisis. These stories illustrate the profound impact that fasting can have in overcoming spiritual battles and achieving breakthrough.

1) **The Fast of Moses (Exodus 34:28)**

One of the earliest examples of fasting in the Bible is found in the life of Moses. When Moses ascended Mount Sinai to receive the Ten Commandments, he fasted for forty days and forty nights (Exodus 34:28). This extended fast was a period of intense spiritual preparation and communion with God, during which Moses received the law that would guide the Israelites.

Moses's fast demonstrates how fasting can be a means of receiving divine revelation and equipping oneself for the spiritual challenges ahead. The law given to Moses on Mount Sinai served as the foundation for Israel's covenant relationship with God, and it was during this time of fasting that Moses was uniquely positioned to receive God's instructions.

2) **The Fast of Daniel (Daniel 10:2-3, 12-14)**
Another powerful example of fasting in the Old Testament is found in the life of Daniel. In Daniel 10, we read that Daniel fasted for three weeks, abstaining from choice food, meat, and wine as he sought understanding and revelation from God (Daniel 10:2-3). During this time, Daniel was engaged in spiritual warfare, as he sought to understand a vision he had received.

In response to Daniel's fasting and prayer, an angel appeared to him, explaining that from the first day Daniel set his heart to humble himself before God, his words were heard. The angel also revealed that he had been delayed for twenty-one days by the "prince of the kingdom of Persia," a spiritual force of opposition, until the archangel Michael came to assist him (Daniel 10:12-14). This passage highlights the role of fasting in overcoming spiritual resistance and gaining insight into God's plans.

3) **The Fast of Elijah (1 Kings 19:8)**
Elijah's fast is another significant example of fasting in the Old Testament. After his dramatic confrontation with the prophets of Baal on Mount Carmel, Elijah fled from Queen Jezebel, who sought to kill him. Exhausted and discouraged, Elijah prayed for God to take his life. Instead, an angel appeared and provided him with food and water, strengthening him for the journey ahead.

Elijah then went on a forty-day fast, traveling to Mount Horeb, where he encountered God in a powerful way (1 Kings 19:8). During this fast, Elijah experienced a deep renewal of his spirit, receiving fresh instructions from God and finding the strength to continue his prophetic ministry. Elijah's fast illustrates how fasting can be a means of spiritual renewal and divine encounter, especially in times of discouragement and fear.

4) The Fast of Nineveh (Jonah 3:5-10)

The story of Nineveh is a profound example of how communal fasting can lead to collective deliverance. When the prophet Jonah reluctantly warned the city of Nineveh of impending judgment, the people responded with repentance and fasting. From the king to the commoners, all of Nineveh fasted and put on sackcloth as a sign of their repentance (Jonah 3:5-10).

In response to their humility and repentance, God relented from the disaster He had planned to bring upon them, sparing the city from destruction. The fast of Nineveh demonstrates the power of fasting to avert judgment and secure mercy from God, even for a wicked and sinful nation.

Practical Steps for Using Fasting as a Weapon in Spiritual Warfare

To wield fasting effectively as a weapon in spiritual warfare, believers must approach it with clear purpose, deep faith, and reliance on God's Word. Scripture shows that fasting, combined with prayer, is a powerful tool for seeking God's intervention and overcoming spiritual obstacles. Here is a framework for how to engage in fasting as part of spiritual warfare:

1) **Identify the Spiritual Battle**

Begin by discerning the spiritual battle or issue you are facing. Whether it's a personal struggle, a stronghold in your life, or an attack on your family or community, pinpointing the nature of the battle is essential. This clarity will focus your prayers and fasting efforts on seeking God's intervention in that specific area. Consider the example of King Jehoshaphat in 2 Chronicles 20, who proclaimed a fast throughout Judah when faced with a vast army. By identifying the enemy and bringing the situation to God, the people of Judah aligned their hearts with His will for victory.

2) Seek God's Guidance and Set a Purpose

Scripture teaches that fasting should always be purposeful and Spirit-led. In times of crisis, God often instructs His people to fast with a clear objective. Before you begin, ask the Holy Spirit to reveal the specific intentions for your fast, whether it's deliverance from sin, clarity in decision-making, or intercession for someone in need. Isaiah 58:6 says, "*Is* this not the fast that I have chosen: to loose the bonds of wickedness, to undo the heavy burdens, to let the oppressed go free, and that you break every yoke?" By setting a clear purpose, you align your fast with God's intentions.

3) Combine Fasting with Prayer and Scripture

Fasting without prayer is simply abstaining from food. To harness its power, combine fasting with dedicated prayer and the Word of God. As you fast, spend intentional time in prayer, asking for God's strength in the spiritual battle. The Bible calls the Word of God the "sword of the Spirit" (Ephesians 6:17). Use this sword by declaring God's promises over your circumstances. For example, when facing fear, you might declare, "God has not given us a spirit of fear, but of power and of love and of a sound mind" (2 Timothy 1:7). Meditating on and speaking Scripture strengthens your spirit and reinforces your prayers.

4) Persevere Through Opposition

Spiritual warfare often involves perseverance. As you fast and pray, you may face increased resistance, distractions, or even spiritual attacks. This is not uncommon; even Jesus faced temptation from Satan during His forty-day fast (Matthew 4:1-11). In such moments, hold firmly to your faith, confident that God is with you and that victory is already won through Christ. James 4:7 encourages us to "resist the devil, and he will flee from you." Stand firm and continue fasting with the assurance that God is fighting on your behalf.

5) Celebrate and Share the Victory

When your fast concludes, celebrate the breakthroughs and victories God has granted. Gratitude is a powerful testimony of God's faithfulness and can inspire others in their own spiritual battles. Share your experiences with others, encouraging them to fast and pray as they seek God's guidance and strength. Revelation 12:11 reminds us that believers overcome "by the blood of the Lamb and by the word of their testimony." By sharing your journey, you strengthen your faith and inspire others to engage in spiritual warfare through fasting.

In spiritual warfare, fasting is not just a weapon but a means of aligning with God's power, wisdom, and guidance. When we humble ourselves, seek His face, and use fasting as a tool of spiritual warfare, God moves mightily on our behalf, leading to transformation and victory. By humbling ourselves before God through fasting and prayer, we can break strongholds, overcome the enemy, and secure divine intervention in our lives. The examples from Scripture demonstrate that fasting is not just an act of self-denial but a deliberate and effective tool for engaging in spiritual battles.

As you incorporate fasting into your spiritual life, remember that you are not alone in the fight. God is with you, and through the power of His Spirit, you can stand firm and experience victory in every area of your life. Whether you are facing personal struggles, seeking deliverance, or fighting for your family or community, fasting is a weapon that can bring about lasting change and breakthrough.

EPILOGUE

As we reach the end of *The Fasting Advantage*, it is clear that fasting is more than a simple act of abstention. It is a profound spiritual discipline, a journey of self-denial that invites believers into deeper intimacy with God and aligns them with His purposes. Through fasting, we touch realms of faith that remain hidden in the ordinary rhythms of life. Fasting enables us to quiet the noise, surrender distractions, and invite God to work in and through us. From the biblical examples in both the Old and New Testaments, we have seen that fasting can transform lives, restore nations, and spark revival. It is a timeless practice that God uses to break strongholds, bring clarity, and usher in breakthrough.

We explored the varied types of fasts, from personal one-day fasts to extended communal fasts that span days or even weeks. Each type has its unique value, whether aimed at personal renewal, corporate repentance, or spiritual warfare. We've learned that fasting is not merely a physical practice but one deeply embedded in the spiritual realm. It shapes us internally, strengthens our spirit, and fosters a lifestyle marked by surrender and trust in God. The physiological benefits—the body's detoxification, cellular repair, and enhanced mental clarity—are a remarkable side effect of the deeper spiritual benefits that fasting offers. Indeed, God has designed our bodies to respond to fasting in ways that renew both the physical and spiritual.

Scripture shows that fasting has always been a vital tool for drawing near to God. Jesus Himself fasted and taught His followers that fasting, combined with prayer, could move mountains, cast out spiritual opposition, and bring them into closer alignment with God's will. Through this book, we have explored how fasting strengthens faith, builds resilience, and brings spiritual renewal. We've also delved into the science behind fasting, discovering how the process supports our health and longevity. It is a unique intersection where spiritual and physical health come together, forming a complete lifestyle of dedication and worship.

In embracing *The Fasting Advantage,* you are stepping into a lineage of faith that spans millennia. You are joining the ranks of saints and believers who have set aside personal comfort for the sake of divine purpose. My hope is that this book has equipped you to understand fasting as a powerful tool for both spiritual growth and personal transformation. Whether you are fasting for breakthrough, healing, clarity, or as a regular practice of devotion, may you find the strength and encouragement to persevere.

Finally, I invite you to apply the principles in this book with intentionality and prayer. Use the *Fasting Companion* resources—book, workbook, and app—to guide your journey. Engage with a community of believers who can support and encourage you. As you pursue this path, may you discover the rich depths of God's presence, experience breakthroughs you've longed for, and gain a newfound strength in your faith. May *The Fasting Advantage* become a way of life, leading you closer to the heart of God and helping you walk in the power, purpose, and renewal that fasting brings.

THE IDEAL SPEAKER FOR YOUR NEXT EVENT!

Any organization that wants to develop its people to win in this area needs to hire Dr. Thando for a keynote and/or workshop training!

To Contact or Book
DR. THANDO SIBANDA
to Speak:
bookings@drthando.com
+14699679089

THE IDEAL COACH (OR CONSULTANT) FOR YOU!

If you're ready to overcome challenges, have major breakthroughs, and achieve higher levels in fasting protocols, then you will love having Dr. Thando Sibanda as your coach!

To Contact
DR. THANDO SIBANDA
Email coaching@drthando.com

ENDNOTES

1   Valter D. Longo and Mark P. Mattson, "Fasting: Molecular Mechanisms and Clinical Application," Cell Metabolism 19, no. 2 (2014): 181-92, https://doi.org/j.cmet.2013.12.008; Ruth E. Patterson and Dorothy D. Sears, "Metabolic Effects of Intermittent Fasting," Annual Review of Nutrition 37 (2017): 371-93. https://doi.org/10.1146/annurev-nutr-071816-064634.

2   "Yoshinori Ohsumi: Facts," The Nobel Prize, 11 Nov. 2024, https://www.nobelprize.org/prizes/medicine/2016/ohsumi/facts/.

3   Jaewon Lee, Kim B. Seroogy, and Mark P. Mattson, "Dietary restriction enhances neurotrophin expression and neurogenesis in the hippocampus of adult mice," Journal of Neurochemistry 80, no. 3 (2002) 253-75. https://doi.org/10.1046/j.0022-3042.2001.00747.x.

4   Luigi Fontana and Linda Partridge, "Promoting health and longevity through diet: from model organisms to humans," Cell 161, no. 1 (2015): 106-18, https://doi.org/10.1016/j.cell/2015.02.020; ***MADEO?

5   Wendy Wisner, "Does Fasting Have Mental Health Benefits?" verywell mind, 30 Mar. 2024, https://www.verywellmind.com/does-fasting-have-mental-health-benefits-8612885.

6   Longo and Mattson, "Fasting," 181-92.

7   John F. Cryan and Timothy G. Dinan, "Mind-altering microorganisms: the impact of the gut microbiota on brain and behaviour," Nature Reviews Neuroscience 13, no. 10 (2010): 701-12, https://doi.org/10.1038/nrn3346.

8   Wisner, "Does Fasting Have Mental Health Benefits?"

9   Alexis Wnuk, "How Does Fasting Affect the Brain?" BrainFacts.org, 13 Jul. 2018, https://www.brainfacts.org/Thinking-Sensing-and-Behaving/Diet-and-Lifestyle/2018/How-Does-Fasting-Affect-the-Brain-071318.

10   Kevin S. Seybold and Peter C. Hill, "The role of religion and spirituality in mental and physical health," Current Directions in Psychological Science 10, no.1 (2001): 21-4, https://doi.org/10.1111/1467-8721.00106.

11   Abdolhossein Bastani et al., "The Effects of Fasting During Ramadan on the Concentration of Serotonin, Dopamine, Brain-Derived Neurotrophic Factor and Nerve Growth Factor," Neurol Int. 23, no. 9 (2017): 7043. https://doi.org/0.4081/ni.2017.7043. PMID: 28713531.

12   John F. Cryan and Timothy G. Dinan, "Mind-altering microorganisms: the impact of the gut microbiota on brain and behaviour," Nature Reviews Neuroscience 13, no. 10 (2010): 701-12, https://doi.org/10.1038/nrn3346.

13 Grant M. Tinsley and Paul M. La Bounty, "Effects of intermittent fasting on body composition and clinical health markers in humans," Nutrition Reviews 73, no.10 (2015): 661-74, https://doi.org/10.1093/nutrit/nuv041.

14 Ruth E. Patterson and Dorothy D. Sears, "Metabolic Effects of Intermittent Fasting," Annual Review of Nutrition 37 (2017): 371-93. https://doi.org/10.1146/annurev-nutr-071816-064634.

15 DC Wilcox et al., "The Okinawa program: how the world's longest-lived people achieve everlasting health," The Journal of the American College of Nutrition 28, no. 4 (2009): 500S-516S.

16 Longo and Mattson, "Fasting," 181-92.

17 Andrew B. Newberg, Neurotheology: How science can enlighten us about spirituality (Columbia University Press, 2018).

18 Andrew B. Newberg and Mark Robert Waldman, How God Changes Your Brain: Breakthrough Findings from a Leading Neuroscientist (New York, NY: Ballantine Books, 2009).

19 Andrew B. Newberg, "The neuroscientific study of spiritual practices," Frontiers in Psychology 5, no. 215 (2014): 215, https://doi.org/10.3389/fpsyg.2014.00215.

20 Alexis E. Clark, "A Literature Review of Neurotheology: How Religion Affects the Brain" (master's thesis, The University of Arizona, 2018), http://hdl.handle.net/10150/630381.

21 Newberg and Waldman, How God Changes Your Brain.

22 Newberg and Waldman, How God Changes Your Brain.

23 Jaewon Lee et. al, "Evidence that brain-derived neurotrophic factor is required for basal neurogenesis and mediates, in part, the enhancement of neurogenesis by dietary restriction in the hippocampus of adult mice," Journal of Neurochemistry 82, no. 6 (2002): 1367-75, https://doi.org/10.1046/j.1471-4159.2002.01085.x.

24 Ewelina Palasz et. al, "BDNF as a Promising Therapeutic Agent in Parkinson's Disease," International Journal of Molecular Sciences 21, no.3 (2020): 1170, https://doi.org/10.3390/ijms21031170.

25 Desiree N. Lavin et al., "Fasting induces an anti-inflammatory effect on the neuroimmune system which a high-fat diet prevents," Obesity 19, no. 8 (2011): 1586-94, https://doi.org/10.1038/oby.2011.73.

26 Vipin Sobti, "Belief in Religiosity, Spiritual Well Being, and Fasting," paper presented at the Fasting and Sustainable Health Conference, December 20-21, 2010.

27 Kirk Bingaman, "The Promise of Neuroplasticity for Pastoral Care and Counseling," Pastoral Psychology 62 (2013): 549-60, https://doi.org/10.1007/s11089-013-0513-0.

28 Eileen Luders et al., "Enhanced Brain Connectivity in Long-term Meditation Practitioners," Neuroimage 57, no. 4 (2011): https//doi.org/10.1016/j.neuroimage.2011.05.075.

29 Newberg and Waldman, How God Changes Your Brain.

30 Luders et al., "Enhanced Brain Connectivity in Long-term Meditation Practitioners."

31 Newberg and Waldman, How God Changes Your Brain.

32 John E. Hall, Guyton and Hall Textbook of Medical Physiology, 13th ed. (Elsevier, 2016).

33 Alan R. Saltiel and C. Ronald Kahn, "Insulin signalling and the regulation of glucose and lipid metabolism, Nature 414 (2001): 799-806.
34 Ronald M. Krauss et al., "Dietary Guidelines for Healthy American Adults: A Statement for Health Professionals From the Nutrition Committee, American Heart Association, Circulation 94, no. 7 (1996): https//doi.org/10.1161/01.CIR.94.7.1795.
35 George F. Cahill, Jr., "Fuel Metabolism in Starvation," Annual Review of Nutrition 26 (2006): 1-22, https://doi.org/10.1146/annurev.nutr.26.061505.111258.
36 Robert K. Murray et al., Harper's Illustrated Biochemistry 26th ed. (McGraw-Hill, 2003).
37 Guenther Boden, "Effects of free fatty acids on gluconeogenesis and glycogenolysis," Life Sciences 72, no. 9 (2003): 977-88, https://doi.org/10.1016/S0024-3205(02) 02350-0.
38 Philip J. Randle, "Metabolic fuel selection: General integration at the whole-body level," Proceedings of the Nutrition Society 57, no. 1 (1995): 317-27, https://doi.org/10.1079/PNS19950057.
39 A. Paoli et al., "Beyond weight loss: A review of the therapeutic uses of very-low-carbohydrate (ketogenic) diets," European Journal of Clinical Nutrition 67, no. 8 (2015), 789-96, https://doi.org/10.1038/ejcn.2013.116.
40 Cahill, "Fuel Metabolism in Starvation."
41 Stephen D. Phennye and Jeff S. Volek, The Art and Science of Low Carbohydrate Living: An Expert Guide to Making the Life-Saving Benefits of Carbohydrate Restriction Sustainable and Enjoyable (Balgowlha, Lismore, AUS: Beyond Obesity, 2011).
42 Daniel Murrell, "Autophagy: What You Need to Know," healthline, 5 May 2023, https://www.healthline.com/health/autophagy.
43 Kian Y. Ho et. al, "Fasting enhances growth hormone secretion and amplifies the complex rhythms of growth hormone secretion in man," The Journal of Clinical Investigation 81, no. 4 (1988): 968-75.
44 Simon Dein and Christopher C.H. Cook, "God put a thought into my mind: the charismatic Christian experience of receiving communications from God," Mental Health, Religion & Culture 18, no. 2 (2015): 97–113, https://doi.org/10.1080/13674676.2014.1002761.
45 Guido Kroemer et al., "Autophagy and the Integrated Stress Response, Molecular Cell 40, no. 2 (2010): 280-93, https://doi.org/10.1016/j.molcel.2010.09.023.
46 Desiree N. Lavin, "Fasting induces an anti-inflammatory effect on the neuroimmune system which a high-fat diet prevents," Obesity 19, no.8 (2013): 1586-94. https://doi.org/10.1038/oby.2011.73.
47 Valter D. Longo et al., Intermittent and periodic fasting, longevity and disease," Nature Aging 1, no. 1 (2021): 47-59, https://doi.org/10.1038/s43587-020-00013-3.
48 Longo and Mattson, "Fasting," 181-92.
49 Daniel Murrell, "Autophagy: What You Need to Know," healthline, 5 May 2023, https://www.healthline.com/health/autophagy.

50 Yahyah Aman et al., "Autophagy in healthy aging and disease," Nature Aging 1 (2021): 634-50, https://doi.org/10.1038/s43587-021-00098-4.

51 Kian Y. Ho et. al, "Fasting enhances growth hormone secretion and amplifies the complex rhythms of growth hormone secretion in man."

52 Longo and Mattson, "Fasting," 181-92.

53 Robert Liardon, God's Generals: The Revivalists (Vol. 3) (New Kensington, PA: Whitaker House, 2008).

54 Liardon, God's Generals.

55 Liardon, God's Generals.

www.ingramcontent.com/pod-product-compliance
Lightning Source LLC
Chambersburg PA
CBHW050905160426
43194CB00011B/2289